WHAT'S THEIR WHY?

EXPLORING MOTIVATION & ENGAGEMENT IN LEARNING

DAREN **WHITE**

Contents

Foreword

Daren White is Academic Technologies Lead for one of the largest Multi-Academy Trusts in the UK and co-leader of GEG UK (Google Educator Group). He is also a very lucky husband and father, a keen sportsman and possesses a very dry sense of humour along with a bucket load of 'dad jokes' that hopefully won't make the final edit!

In this book he aims to share the benefit of his experience, his successes and failures and challenges us to consider how we might make education both more engaging, looking at motivation, curriculum design, teaching and learning approaches and useful tools.

A teacher of Spanish, French and numerous other subjects over a period of 23 years, Daren has a wealth of experience as a classroom teacher and pastoral leader as well as a successful senior leader with experience in leading schools from Special Measures to Outstanding.

In recent times Daren has turned his attention to the use of technology in schools, both in the classroom and beyond and has a substantial social media presence. Daren wrote a number of ebooks during the COVID pandemic to support teachers around the globe in delivering online lessons and led extensive training through in person events and online on a global scale.

Daren is a Certified Google Trainer, Coach and Innovator and as his VIA20 Innovator he developed myedtechbuddy.co.uk to help build confidence using technology for learning.

Daren has also had the honour of presenting at ISTE events and the Bett Show in London and in 2022 was named in the #Edtech50 list.

You can follow Daren on Twitter, LinkedIn and Youtube as well as via GEG UK.

December 2022

The History

The last few years have seen more rapid changes in education that we have seen in more than the previous 200 years. The colossal impact of COVID 19 globally is well documented and education took a battering for all manner of reasons. Whether it be falling attendance and/or rising persistent absence, lack of access through deprivation, long-term effects of COVID or simply the change in what had become established routines, the changes came thick and fast. And yet, almost without exception, teachers across the world pulled together and delivered the best quality education they could in these highly challenging and rapidly changing circumstances.

I can vividly recall the week prior to the first lockdown in March 2020, chatting with a colleague about what might happen if schools were unable to function normally. Sadly, I still feel the need to explain that schools never actually closed despite the many headlines and outpourings on social media to the contrary. I can honestly say that in actual fact, throughout the pandemic, the schools I was involved with were actually open more than normal as we provided early starts, later finishes and even school holiday provision to accommodate the children of key workers who were needed on the front line as well as the vulnerable.

It was that chat with my colleague that got us thinking about how we might provide some pretty urgent and extensive, yet accessible, training for staff who were not overly confident with technology in the classroom, let alone using it from home for remote learning. We drew up a rough plan but honestly didn't think it would get to that point.

Cut to the Friday afternoon and the news came that from Monday, England would be in lockdown and the majority of learning would have to take place online in some form. Call it foresight, call it luck but whatever it was, we were ready and by the Monday morning we were offering daily training for colleagues across all of our schools. The feedback received from grateful colleagues helped shape our offer moving forward and we embarked on a journey to eventually providing live lessons to all pupils all day. Ok, this wasn't a quick journey by any means, some of us were experimenting with live lessons quite early on and through our own successes and failures, we were able to learn, adapt and advise the best methods available depending on each teacher's situation.

It's easy to forget that for many teachers, they had their own children at home while they were working and that can make for some interesting video calls, as of course can the hugely popular 'pet bombs' that became commonplace at both ends of the virtual line.

I have very fond memories of students joining lessons with their dogs and cats and it proved a great way to get pupils to open up and chat to each other. At that point I had 2 cats, Maureen who doesn't speak to anyone, and Alan, who is a big fan of video meetings and laptop keys. Alan's typing skills along with the occasional visit from the chickens from the garden kept me on my toes to say the least but it also kept the pupils interested. They were getting to see their teachers in 'real life' even if only virtually. For some, realising their teachers had families, pets and lives outside school was a revelation and they became naturally inquisitive.

For this reason, whenever I taught a lesson online, we always took some time to ask each other what we'd been up to and how we were feeling. I'm a strong believer in being open and honest and was happy to share my own mental challenges when the appropriate opportunities arose. The more we did it, the more I found pupils began joining lessons early for a chat. In one case, joining to give me a tour of their newly refitted kitchen and to meet their Mum, who had been listening in to lessons while completing her own work from home. Mum wanted to try out some Spanish she'd picked up and she did great!

Although it was undoubtedly a very challenging time for everyone, not least those who sadly lost loved ones as a result of COVID but I have to confess to having enjoyed at least some part of it. With the rule book not yet written for online teaching, it opened up a world of creativity that I believe has been long absent from classrooms and corridors all over the world.

The constantly changing circumstances, locations and access issues forced us to rethink how we might deliver our content in an engaging and impactful way but the lockdown also gave us the time to think too. That is often the part that is missing from busy school days of back to back lessons, break duty, lunch clubs and meetings. I strongly believe that everyone should have an opportunity each day to switch off from everything else, step back and constructively reflect on their work. Sadly, more often than not we are teaching all day, not drinking anywhere near enough water for fear of having to go to the loo mid-lesson, eating our lunch during a club or detention (if we are lucky) and then, when the hard graft of the day is done and the pupils go home, we get to sit in meetings when our brains are either fried or spiritually already 30 miles down the road.

It's this hectic nature of education, especially in the UK, that has led us to where we were just prior to COVID. And where were we? Well, not much further ahead than where we were in the 1800s.

Compare two classrooms and the differences are negligible, whilst the similarities are nothing short of embarrassing.

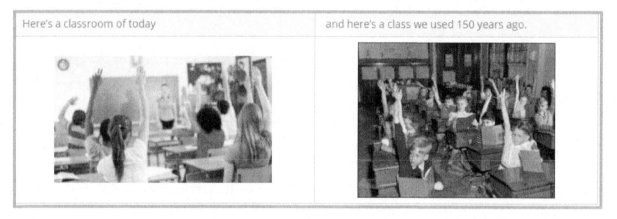

| Here's a classroom of today | and here's a class we used 150 years ago. |

This is a photo brought to you by Peycho's Blog, showing that the structure of a classroom has not changed over the last 150 years.

Ok, this is just one example but it's not unfamiliar right? I've been fortunate to teach in a number of new builds in recent years and the excitement around them is palpable, however, in reality there is little thought about teaching and learning when these new builds are designed. The focus is more on maximising the use of space and making sure you can get upwards of 30 in the room. There is often very little flexibility in terms of layout, equipment, furnishings and in some cases, everything is decided by the proximity of power sockets, not by the optimum environment for learning.

If you are working in schools where a new building is on the cards, I urge you to get involved in the conversations as early as possible in the vain hope that you might get some say in how your teaching space looks.

Personally, I have always been of the opinion that the teacher does not need to be the expert in the classroom. Yes, subject knowledge is obviously important, but none of us can accurately know and remember everything that might arise, particularly if we are inspiring probing questions from our pupils.

If then, the teacher is not so much the knowledge expert but more the skills expert, there is no good reason for the teacher to be at the front of the class and it certainly doesn't mean that they have to be where the plugs are. We've got that completely the wrong way round.

The Now

I find myself writing this as we are approaching 2023 and of course, everyone has embraced the 'new normal' or maybe not so much.

The huge cognitive load that teachers went through to completely change their day to day way of working massively took its toll. Add to this the constant interruptions of further lockdowns, rule changes, continued absences and long-term effects of COVID and teachers are exhausted.

In 23 years I've never experienced colleagues who are so tired from the constant battle of TAGs, recovery curriculums, interventions and cover. Add to that the ever shrinking budgets and pay rises announced after schools had submitted their budgets and you can see why so many are on their knees.

We all know colleagues who are teaching 24 out of 25 hours a week and then having to use their weekends and evenings to complete their marking and assessment, develop curriculum maps, prepare for Deep Dives and more. It's simply not sustainable and that's why recruitment and retention is in crisis.

I liken the constant scrutiny of schools by Ofsted, Performance Measures, League Tables and recruitment problems to that of a Premier League football manager. It doesn't matter what you've done in the past, you're only as good as your last set of results and those stakes are incredibly high!

I have tremendous empathy and admiration for Headteachers who are spinning so many plates (that they can't afford to replace if they break) whilst also trying to remain visible around school and approachable to staff and students. They are true heroes in my mind. Most of us have scarcely an idea what they are dealing with day in, day out. Leading a school is a lonely job, perhaps one of the loneliest thanks to the competitive nature of league tables, numbers on roll and budgets. If you do one thing tomorrow, ask your Headteacher how they are. They'll appreciate it for sure.

Anyway, I digress. We're now back in the classrooms and in many instances teachers have held on to some of what they learned during the periods of remote learning. I am certainly seeing more collaboration, more use of interactive tools such as Jamboard and Miro as well as a resurgence in the popularity of visualisers.

The biggest change for me has been in the methods used to give feedback to students with much more of a drive towards using rubrics, verbal feedback and even video feedback through screencasting. The reason? They are easy to use, they save huge amounts of time **and** they actually improve the quality of the feedback given at the same time as making them more accessible.

We'll take a look at some of my favourite tools in later chapters.

On the flip side though, there is also evidence that some of what we learned from remote learning and some of the aspects that certain groups of pupils really thrived on are already being forgotten.

Consider that one pupil who is a little introverted and doesn't like to share their opinion or ideas in class. During lockdown, many of these pupils thrived in having the luxury of answering via an app or a Google form where other pupils couldn't see their answer, thus taking away the jeopardy of making mistakes. Where they thrived, others struggled and vice versa, but back in the classroom we all too often revert to what we feel more comfortable or confident with and that pupil loses out.

What about those pupils who can't learn with distractions around them but thrived when working from home? What do we do for them now?

I was fortunate to be the Edtech Demonstrator Program Delivery Lead for our trust over the last 2 years and I have to say, it was an absolute delight working with other schools and trusts to look at how they could implement a digital strategy and upskill their stakeholders.

As a result of this work, along with other Edtech Demonstrators, we were asked to submit a report to the Department of Education based on our findings and the future of digital maturity in education.

As a team we worked long and hard to produce a report that not only talked the talk, but also walked the walk. We crafted a passionate, highly detailed and interactive Genially presentation demonstrating the approaches we recommend as well as highlighting the evidence in support of it. We were all really excited at the prospect of shaping the future of digital education in England and felt truly empowered. The one thing we all agreed on was that there is never going to be a case for one size fits all approaches.

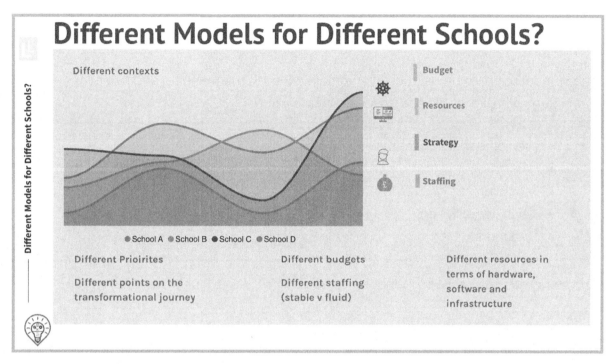

Taken from the report: The Path to Digital Maturity by Edtech Demonstrator Partners

We waited, and then we received a request...

"Can you please provide a PDF copy that we can print and share with the Department?"

Whoosh! Away went that rug from under us.

Having taken on board the audience, we reluctantly agreed to provide what was requested but did stress the importance of seeing the presentation in its intended, interactive state. I would love to have been a fly on the wall to see how it was shared in the end. I can probably guess though.

The review of the Edtech Demonstrator Program is still ongoing at time of writing but we are hoping for a detailed report and recommendations soon. It will be fascinating to see if any or our ideas make the final cut.

At the Bett Show 2022 at London's Excel, the DfE announced their new Digital Standards for education.

To quote the Digital Standards directly:
"These standards should be used as **guidelines** to support your school or college use the right digital infrastructure and technology. More digital and technology categories will be added to the service.

Meeting them can help you make more informed decisions about technology leading to safer, more cost-efficient practices and new learning opportunities for students.

The standards are to be used by everyone involved in the planning and use of technology within schools and colleges, including:

- senior leadership teams
- IT staff
- suppliers
- technical advisers
- teachers

The standards can help your school or college with:

- budgeting for technology procurement and maintenance
- buying technology equipment and services
- renewing a contract with a technology provider to ensure their purchases meet your needs
- correctly installing new equipment"

Whilst this is well intentioned, in reality schools are already struggling to make ends meet thanks to unfunded pay rises and the cost of living crisis, added to potentially years of underinvestment. Many of the recommendations require a huge investment both in infrastructure and in time.

There are lots of recommendations but very little in the way of advice on how to bring them to life. The fact that the stated deadlines are "as soon as you can" seems to confirm the fact that in reality, schools aren't going to be able to do this any time soon and certainly not without funding and support.

One aspect of the recommendations for immediate implementation (if possible) is the use of MFA (multi-factor authentication).

The current guidance states:

"Where practical, you must enable multi-factor authentication. This should always include cloud services for non-teaching staff. All staff are **strongly encouraged** to use multi-factor authentication.

Ask users for a second authentication factor when accessing sensitive data. For example, when moving from a lesson plan to financial or personal data.

Multi-factor authentication should include at least 2 of the following:

- passwords constructed in the formats described earlier in standard 3
- a managed device, that may belong to the organisation
- an application on a trusted device
- a device with a trusted network IP address, you should not use this in MFA for accounts with administrator rights or for accessing sensitive data
- a physically separate token
- a known/trusted account, where a second party authenticates another's credentials
- a biometric test"

Now this raises some particular challenges depending on your school and your personal circumstances.

Enabling MFA often requires a second device, usually a mobile phone to receive codes via SMS or an authenticator app. The first, of course, is dependent on phone signal in your area and the second on the type of mobile phone you own (if you own one).

The second issue here is also around the use of mobile devices in the classroom. This is a real Marmite point for many in education and for parents.

In many schools across the country the use of mobile devices in the classroom is banned completely for students and for adults, which is obviously problematic when required to authenticate on login.

In other schools, the use of mobiles is by teacher discretion and poses less of an issue but you can already see a divide emerging.

I can see the value of both approaches and again, it's horses for courses based on each school's unique situation but I'm firmly in the 'teach responsible use' camp as opposed to a blanket ban. In my opinion, teaching users to take responsibility for how and when they use devices is a life skill and one they won't develop innately, but more on that later perhaps.

Ultimately, we have a series of Digital Standards that are actually just guidance. We don't have the support guidance from the DfE for how to best achieve these standards and in many cases, schools are relying on a single IT Technician, split across a number of sites to lead the way in amongst firefighting the day to day of IT Technical Support.

As my good friend Abid Patel recently stated, if the DfE is serious about these Standards, then funds must be provided and ring fenced for their implementation. Keeping users, and especially children safe online should never be a postcode lottery but the reality is that without dedicated funding, we won't get parity, especially at a time when some schools are turning off the heating to make ends meet.

The Future

We've all seen statistics quoted about the percentage of jobs that don't exist yet and we can argue the toss on that until the cows come home. The simple fact is that for our pupils, the reality is that by 2030 many of the jobs that currently exist may not and many new ones certainly will.

What is also certain is that 'careers for life' trends are decreasing and a large proportion of job mobility (moving from one job to another) result in a complete change of field, role or environment.

Google for Education recently published Part 1 of a new report: The Future of Education (Google for Education) in which they identified the top 3 trends in global employment.

Trend 1: Rising demand for global problem solvers

Trend 2: Change in the skill sets required for work

Trend 3: Shift to a lifelong learning mindset

The World Economic Forum, in its Future of Jobs report (2020), identified these five skills as the most in-demand among employers globally, by 2025:

- ***Analytical thinking and innovation*** | The capacity to solve novel, ill-defined problems in the real world.

- ***Active learning and learning strategies*** | Understanding of the implications of new information for both current and future problem-solving and decision-making.

- ***Complex problem-solving*** | Abilities that influence the acquisition and application of knowledge in problem-solving.

- ***Critical thinking and analysis*** | Using logic and reasoning to identify the strengths and weaknesses of alternative solutions, conclusions or approaches to problems, as well as assessing performance of yourself, other individuals or organisations to make improvements or take corrective action.

- ***Creativity, originality and initiative*** | Capacity to analyse information and use logic to address issues and problems, apply alternative thinking to develop new, original ideas and answers.

As educators, we have to shift our thinking and understand that educating for jobs is a thing of the past. Now and into the future we need to educate pupils on how to learn to create their future, to create their job.

Content can and does become irrelevant (take recent historical discoveries for example where we're having to unlearn what we were taught was true because of new evidence). Skills however are transferable and stand you in good stead for future challenges.

Jobs that don't exist yet (at time of writing)

Commercial Space Pilot

With global warming on the rise, the likes of Jeff Bezoz and Elon Musk are investing heavily in the space travel sector. With tourism, inevitably comes commerce and pilots will be needed to fly supply craft to and from the International Space Station or wherever we may end up visiting.

Work From Home Coordinator

Post COVID, more and more organisations are flexing to remote or hybrid working to reduce bills and improve employee wellbeing. However, this change requires experts in health, safety, ergonomics and mental health to ensure businesses can not only survive but thrive while working in pyjamas.

Work From Home Coordinators might draft remote working policies, checking remote Health and Safety implications such as desk height, screen position and ventilation as well as ensuring employees are physically and mentally well while doing their jobs at home.

Human-Machine Teaming Manager

Ok, so robots aren't taking over the world, but they are doing some amazing things in the workplace. However, the humans around them are equally important and companies will need managers to create a synergy between the machines and the people so that they can work collaboratively, effectively and safely.

Esports Coach

As the popularity of esports continues to grow, and more and more NGBs (National Governing Body) embrace virtual tournaments, the stakes will be raised exponentially, as will the financial reward for participation in esports events. Therefore, the demand for esport coaches to help individuals maximise their performance is a natural progression.

Whatever happens in the next decade and beyond, we can all agree that versatility is going to be a highly prized commodity.

So the question is, how might we redesign education to equip young people for a successful future?

Redesigning or Redefining Education

It would be very easy to gather groups of experts together, see what's worked before and come up with a rebadged version of the same diet, but no-one in their right mind would do that, right?

Instead it's vital that we strip everything back and ask ourselves some key questions, starting with why?

Why do we teach pupils?
Why do we teach them what we teach?
Why do we teach it when we do?
Why do we teach it in the way we do?

We have to define our purpose before we embark on this voyage or we'll end up in exactly the same place we always do.

There are some great examples around the world of schools and systems that have been radically redesigned with excellent effect and all using very distinct and brave approaches. I'm not pretending that changing the entire education system isn't hard, but nobody ever really discovered anything new by sticking to what's easy.

Some examples from around the world that you might want to investigate further:

Agora Schools
If you've not already come across Agora Schools strap yourself in!

Agora is **"the school with no classes, no classrooms and no curriculum"**.

At Agora, the journey starts with the pupil. What do they want to learn? What are their talents, interests, and ambitions?

Pupils are encouraged to "use everything in the world that's worthwhile to investigate, make or develop as [their] personal starting point for learning". A personal coach supports and supervises the learning process. At Agora they traded courses, timetables, classes, and tests for challenges, collaboration and coaching by teachers.

At Agora, we believe that school has to be a good mix between:

Harvard University ... a place where all the knowledge of the world is within reach.

A Buddhist monastery ... where you feel comfortable and at ease and where you discover what is valuable to you in life.

A creative laboratory ... where you can make and try everything you can imagine: painting, welding, graphic design, 3D printing...from cooking to programming to making a robot: if you can imagine it, you can make it.

A marketplace ... where you can see new things, meet and inspire each other, debate and interact.

Disneyland ... a place where you feel happy, amazed and above all: welcome, supported and challenged by the staff!!

This bold statement underpins the culture of innovation and versatility that permeates throughout.

Pupils at Agora benefit from a personal workspace and a coach group that consists of around 15 other pupils of different ages and levels. In their coaching group pupils have a personal workspace which they can customise and arrange to their own taste and there are some incredibly imaginative spaces that are truly inspiring. This means there is no walking to a different classroom every hour.

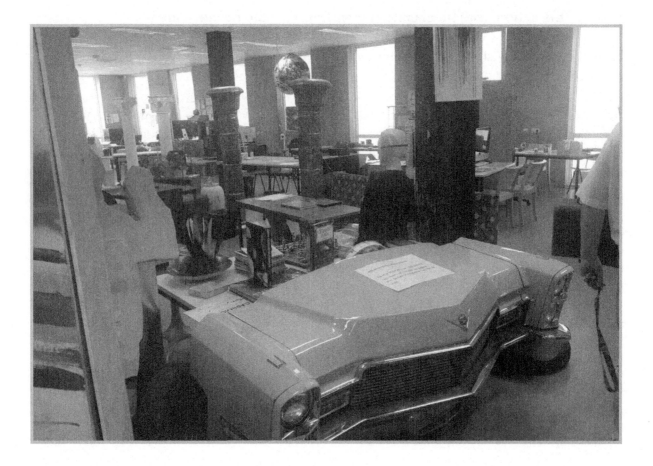

Personal Workspaces at Agora. Credit: https://petermerry.org/

The first few weeks at Agora involves an intense unlearning bootcamp where pupils unlearn all the expectations they already have of a school. Pupils are openly told "We are not going to teach you. You are going to learn to teach yourselves".

The coach's job is to help the pupils in their coach group follow their learning passion, signpost what they are learning and why and offer them ideas and opportunities to make their personal and educational development more holistic.

Coaching groups meet at the start of every day with a discussion around an item that is in the news. Everyone also enjoys 30 minutes of silent focus time each day.

Here, all learning happens through challenges which pupils determine themselves. Their coach documents the competencies they are developing and demonstrating in a rigorous digital platform that parents can also access. Pupils at Agora are given a guarantee that they **will** pass the exam they want to pass in the traditional number of years it would take, **or less**.

Flexibility is key at Agora but so is responsibility. There are also dedicated workspaces where pupils can cook, do carpentry, painting, metalworking, program a robot, and more. A team of volunteers from the community and companies also offer inspirational sessions which pupils can join. Mobile phone use is ubiquitous. Pupils are encouraged to make the appropriate choices around what to use and for what purpose, in order to complete their learning plans for the week and ultimately succeed.

I know if I were offered this opportunity as a child I would have grabbed it with both hands. If I were recruiting, I'd have no hesitation about employing someone who had that sort of educational background, they would be your planners, your coordinators, your doers and your creators. They will likely be mentally agile, knowledgeable but equally skillful, having learnt through more experiential approaches than theoretical.

Agora School - not a traditional 'classroom' in sight but plenty of learning.

Sweden

Another example of large scale educational transformation can be found in Sweden where the main objectives of the National Digitalisation Strategy is to create further opportunities for digitalisation, achieve a high level of digital competence, and promote the development of knowledge and equal opportunities and access to technology.

The strategy focuses on 3 main areas, each accompanied by a set of sub-goals.
- Digital competence for everyone, pupils, staff and leaders.
- Equal access and use, including technical infrastructure & pedagogical support
- Research into the possibilities of digitalisation

Regional procurement forms part of this strategy and helps to both standardise opportunities and offers economies of scale in terms of product purchase as well as training and use. Teacher voice and choice also play a major factor in the procurement process.

Uruguay

Now Uruguay might not be the first country that springs to mind when considering educational change. This small south american country however has taken bold steps in their digital transformation journey. The national virtual educational program, Plan Ceibal, was put in place long before COVID, in 2007. This project aimed to connect to high-speed internet those pupils who otherwise wouldn't show up on screen and it paid off during the recent disruptions.

By 2012, the World Bank confirmed that Uruguay had provided all 300,000 students in the country's public schools with their own computer. These devices, handed out to pupils alongside free internet access meant that all pupils can make use of them at school and can take them home, benefiting them but also their wider families. These devices are updated on a 3 year cycle, depending on educational needs.

So how is it, that a decade on from then, in the UK we still can't make the same claim about either devices or internet access?

Norway

At the start of the millennium, Norway experienced some "Pisa Shame" which sparked a reform of education. Within 3 years, paper-based national tests were introduced to address new testing and accountability policies and then in 2008 they were digitised by Inspera. Now digital assessment is running throughout, from primary to Higher Ed.

In 2016, the Norwegian government published its digital agenda, making the use of ICT in education <u>a priority</u>.

With the Scandinavian landscape made up of small nations with large regional differences, it was imperative to acknowledge the diverse needs of learners as well as the diverse cultures from which they are drawn.

This digital assessment approach allows the focus to remain firmly on the core purpose of delivering pedagogical benefits to teachers and pupils.

When you then consider that educational budgets are ring fenced and that the use of artificial intelligence to tailor learning tasks based on performance, it's easy to see why, both in 2006 and 2012, Norway was ahead of the EU average when it came to the use of computers in the classroom.

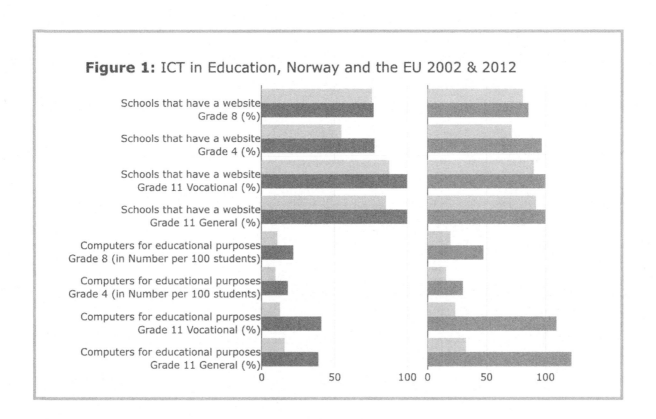

Figure 1: ICT in Education, Norway and the EU 2002 & 2012

Source: European Commision. Digital Agenda

This kind of innovative thinking, and more importantly, action is key to changing the fortunes of our young people.

If time travel were accessible (notice I'm not saying possible) I'm confident you could create a Channel 4 type TV series of Teacher Swap with teachers from the

1900s swapping places with 'modern' counterparts. However, I suspect the main difference from the standard Wife Swap or Rich House, Poor House format would likely be that the Victorian teachers would cope perfectly well in a 'modern' classroom and most 'modern' teachers would cope perfectly well in a Victorian classroom. The simple fact is we have been teaching in very similar ways for around 200 years, but in the overall scheme of things, 200 years is not a very long time.

We don't know it all.

We don't yet know the best ways to teach or learn.

We only know the best ways we've discovered so far, and for certain individuals and circumstances.

That's why we must continue to embrace innovation and reimagine education. We owe it to our young people.

Hopefully we can all agree that every child has the right to the same opportunities and experiences regardless of circumstances. It should never be acceptable that pupils might miss out because of their location or circumstances. If we are to truly continue to deliver the best experiences for all our pupils, we have to continually ask the question:

"What's their why?"

What motivates them?
What engages them?
Why do they come to school every day?
What are they hoping to gain?

Once we establish that, and it might not be easy to do in some cases, we can begin to ensure our own why is in alignment.

The why?

Pupil Voice is one of those buzzwords that feels like it's been around forever, but rarely have I seen anything sustained and embedded. I think partly, this is down to leadership. I don't mean lack of leadership, I mean a lack of consistent leadership. In my own experience and from conversations with others including many young people over the years, Pupil Voice is often given a 'push' at different times by different staff members assigned to the task. In the best cases these staff are passionate about the power of Pupil Voice, in the worst cases they are sadly paying lip service or box-ticking in order to fulfil UPS standards of whole school impact. Therefore, the vision for Pupil Voice in school is often subjective. Whether it's the lead staff member or the pupils involved, quite often they have little more than 2 or 3 terms to make an impact before they 'move on'.

As a result, momentum suffers and therefore so does the value and the impact. I've always believed Pupil Voice is important both in terms of the common themes like what to call the class pet or how to improve the toilets or the canteen food, but also in terms of teaching and learning.

Throughout my career I've been fortunate to interview many candidates for teaching and non-teaching roles and the occasions when pupil voice was incorporated have often resulted in the better appointments. I know there are some who disagree with pupil interview panels but in my own experience they can be a fascinating insight, not just into the candidates but also into the minds of the young people as they decide what questions to ask. We always allowed them to draw up their own questions and the pupil interviews took the form of informal chats that formed part of the more formal makeup of an interview day.

Pupil's opinions on suitable candidates were always sought and we always fed back to the pupil panel, whether their choices matched our own or not. Pupils said they appreciated this and of course, they took some ownership of their education experience.

I've never been a fan of formal observations, which is not great when you've been teaching for over 23 years and have been through more than 20, yes 20 Ofsted inspections plus several 'Mocksteds' throughout that time. I know it's a contentious issue: some people thrive on being observed. Some love an unannounced observation, others like a bit of warning. For me, it didn't matter, I hated all forms and more often than not, overthought, overplanned or over-adapted things trying to jump through whichever hoops were popular at the time. I wonder how many of us have been told at some point that our lesson was inadequate because everyone was doing the same task, regardless of the outcomes? What we should have been asking is how were all pupils managing to do the same task given their different abilities, motivations and starting points?

I am firmly in the camp that regular conversations with pupils about their learning is the best gauge of how well a teacher is performing. Yes, you have to be subjective, but in general I have always found pupils to be quite reasonable and honest, even if they don't particularly like a subject or get on with a member of staff.

So, if we can ask how things are going, who they'd like as their teacher, how often chips should be on the menu, why aren't we asking more often about what motivates them?

Well, you've guessed it, the answer is most probably time. These conversations take time, but they need to be conversations. A blanket careers survey for example, just won't cut it. You won't get the nuances and the reasons behind their answers, you won't get to challenge and expand on them and that's where you find the golden nuggets!

Imagine you are starting a new school year but this year there is no pressure at all to deliver curriculum for the first few days. The priority for everyone is to settle in and to get to know your pupils, whether they be reception age or Year 11.

What would you **choose** to do during that time?
What would pupils **choose** to do during that time?

Why not try asking some of your current pupils what they would choose? You might be pleasantly surprised and even inspired by their response.

The fact is, given the time, we would probably all do things a lot differently. We might be more creative in our methods, we might delve deeper into certain aspects of a topic that sparks interest, we might go off on a complete tangent because it's interesting and relevant, even if it's not on the schema or the assessment for this term. Imagine that!

Research has shown that people who are intrinsically motivated tend to be more successful in later life than those who are more extrinsically motivated. Of course, this makes sense as the intrinsically motivated often seek out further opportunities to better themselves or their understanding and skills. Just take David Beckham for example, who spent hours and hours on the training ground as a youngster taking free kicks and then continued to do so in his professional career despite being one of the best in the world. Did he do all that practice because he wanted a badge, a certificate or a pat on the back? No, he did it because he wanted to be the best.

Leaders spend a lot of time in schools tinkering with reward policies to motivate young people, and of course, you have to do this because the nature of a school's pupil population is constantly evolving. What motivates one class or year group may have zero, or worse, a negative impact on another. If we were to survey all schools I reckon we've probably tried everything between us, but what worked for some won't work for others or might work at one point in time but not another.

Throughout my time in education, here are some of the incentives I remember:

As a teacher
- Merit stickers in Pupil planners
- Class merits (I used to buy my tutor group donuts every time they got to 25)
- Certificates
- Fast Passes for the lunch queue
- Class parties or trips to Bowling
- Sweets
- Hot Chocolate with the Head
- Letter from the Head
- Reward Trips to theme parks
- Lapel badges
- Positive and negative points on our MIS
- Trophies and Awards

As a pupil
- Commendations - my teachers would write "Commendation" on our work and my tutor would take a tally each week. We rarely knew why we got the commendation though.

That's it as a pupil. Ok, admittedly it was a while ago but that's all I can remember. I don't even recall what happened with the totals that were collected.

I guess I'm fortunate that I am probably biassed toward the intrinsic side overall and have always strived to improve off my own back. That's not saying extrinsic motivators didn't work for me. They absolutely did, particularly in the Cubs and latterly the Scouts when I was proud to wear my uniform and display my arm and chest full of badges. Luckily I have long arms.

I don't honestly feel though that the extrinsic rewards of school had any impact on me, aside from the jeopardy of exam results, if you can call those rewards. In fact, looking back, I would often create my own challenges and reward myself for achieving them.

I was quite a keen mathematician at school and would often complete additional work from my Y books at home. So much so that I completed Y5 (the Year 11 book) but the end of Year 10. I was like a young Carol Vorderman at that point but without the Rear of the Year accolades. I was super pleased to have completed the books and eager to let my teacher know so that I could get some further challenge. Unfortunately, this was 1991/92 and stretch and challenge usually involved sitting me with Freddie to keep him focused and help him with his work. In this case though, Freddie wasn't in top set so I was issues with a maths book the size of the Yellow Pages* and told to work though that and then check the answers in the back. With the best will and self-control in the world at age 14 I can freely admit to sticking to the questions first, answers after approach for all of about 2 weeks. I was bored stiff in maths for most of Year 11 and only got a B in the end as I was out of practice. In a way though, the experience was useful to some extent as I am now pretty good at reverse thinking a problem from a solution.

Another example that springs to mind was in English. We had two teachers, married to each other, but strangely I only got on with one of them. When it came to writing essays I would pull out all the stops for the one I liked and for the other, I would challenge myself to fit as many words onto an A4 side of paper as I possibly could, just to make it harder for them to read. I recall my record being well over 500 words and me being slightly unpopular. I didn't care though because I'd achieved my aim.

*Yellow Pages is like the internet in a book. Handy for finding phone numbers or reaching things on high shelves.

Dopamining

This may not be a term you are familiar with, but it's one that I now realise I am guilty of. It's a major factor in motivation, reward, performance and mental health and is therefore, important for us to consider when devising approaches to teaching and learning for people of all ages. So what exactly is Dopamine and why is it relevant to learning?

Dopamine is a neurotransmitter that helps send signals in the brain and is involved in controlling movement, amongst other things. Dopamine plays a vital role in the brain's reward system, helping to reinforce certain behaviours that result in reward. A dopamine surge is what prompts a laboratory rat to repeatedly press a lever to get food, or a human to devour a whole packet of biscuits.

Recent scientific research also suggests that dopamine can help with unlearning fearful associations and is now being utilised to help people with anxiety disorders, such as phobias or PTSD.

More so, Dopamine also aids the flow of information to the brain regions responsible for thought and emotion. According to the Cleveland Clinic, too much or too little dopamine — or problems in the way the brain uses dopamine — may play a role in disorders such as schizophrenia or attention deficit hyperactivity disorder (ADHD).

In other parts of the body, dopamine acts as a type of hormone called catecholamine. Catecholamines are made in the adrenal glands — small hormone production factories that sit on top of the kidneys.

There are three main catecholamines: Dopamine, Epinephrine (adrenaline) and Norepinephrine.

These hormones are into the bloodstream when the body is physically or mentally stressed, causing biochemical changes that stimulate the amygdala, the part of our primordial brain linked to survival instincts, thus activating the so-called fight-or-flight response. In reality, the body's natural reaction to real or perceived stress can be categorised as the 4 Fs: Fight, Flight, Flock and Freeze.

These are the 4 instinctive reactions when the primitive brain perceives fear. Whether you're a caveman faced with a predator or a child put on the spot to answer a question in class, any of the 4 Fs can be triggered without any conscious thought on your part.

The 4 Fs	Prehistoric Cave dweller facing down a predator	Child in a modern classroom asked to answer a question
Fight (defiance)	Attack the predator	Outright refusal to answer
Flight (escape the situation)	Run away	Storm out, Ask to go to the toilet
Flock (normalising, safety in numbers)	Gather others for reassurance	Look to others who feel and react the same
Freeze (physically or emotionally paralysed)	Physically unable to move	Says nothing at all

Dopamine receptors are proteins found in the brain and nerves throughout the body. These receptors are the nerve cells' chemical receivers. Dopamine molecules bind to the receptor and set off chemical reactions.

As a dopamine signal approaches a nearby neuron, it attaches to that neuron's receptor. The receptor and neurotransmitter work like a lock and key. The dopamine attaches to the dopamine receptor, delivering its chemical message by causing changes in the receiving nerve cell.

These dopamine receptors play an important role in movement, coordination, fine motor skills, pleasure, cognition, memory, and learning.

Any abnormal change to these dopamine receptors in the brain can cause nerve cells to release too much dopamine or prevent the nervous system from recycling dopamine once it's done its job, hijacking the brain's inbuilt reward system. These abnormal changes can be caused by certain antidepressant or anti-anxiety medications and street drugs such as methamphetamines, cocaine and heroin.

Dopamine creates feelings of pleasure, therefore large amounts of dopamine flooding our system produces a "high" that leaves us wanting more. Just like with drugs, individuals can build up a tolerance to rewards and in order to achieve these pleasurable highs, require an increase in the stimulant.

This is one of the main reasons why fixed reward systems in schools need to adapt. What stimulates a dopamine reaction in a Year 5 pupil differs greatly from that which might stimulate a Year 10, so we have to be prepared for some flexibility, making pupil voice even more valuable. Finding out what rewards pupils might want is a great exercise and might even throw up some heartwarming surprises.

If we don't provide the correct stimulus and rewards our pupils will go dopamining for themselves, seeking out alternative ways to get that "high", and more often than not, in ways that are not conducive to a learning environment. We have to know our pupils, know what drives them and know what they want to achieve.

As key parts of an education system, working towards the same goals, we should at least know what those goals are, and they ought not be purely ones imposed for the purpose of leagues tables and inspections.

Take EYFS for example. Now, my daughter is now 18 so it's been while since I was at a parents evening in reception class, looking like a 6'5 grizzly sat on a tiny chair, but bear with me. (See what I did there?)

In EYFS we encourage learning through play, through experience, through making mistakes and trial and error. We focus on kindness and sharing and being a good friend. Creativity is front and centre and outcomes are deemed less important than the learning process. Let's face it, nothing on our fridge doors is going to win a Turner Prize but the fact of them being there acts as a daily reminder to our children that we are proud of their achievements. Whoosh! Here comes a dopamine rush.

As we move pupils through Primary this continues until the pressure of SATs kick in, let alone 11+. As parents clamber to buy study guides, practice workbooks and book tutors to boost their child's performance in the exams, the fun and playfulness is lost, giving way to anxiety and stress. It's little wonder we have a mental health crisis amongst our young people and it can't all be blamed on social media and peer pressures. We have to take some responsibility for the situation we find ourselves in, even though we may not be in a position to affect much change. As we impose our goals on our children, we can also impose our success criteria - but these don't often result in the dopamine rush our young people seek.

By the time pupils arrive at Secondary, these confident Year 6 pupils who have held positions of responsibility in class and across the school, have led assemblies, welcomed visitors and supported younger pupils in the playground; those that have been interrupting their game at breaktime to make sure someone is ok because they saw them alone at the Friendship Stop, are suddenly swatted like flies.

"We're sitting in rows", "Where are you going?", "Sit back down", "No you can't go to the toilet", "Stop running in the playground" - almost sung in chorus like a football chant for at least the first term until all the energy is drummed out of them. Many of the dopamine highs they used to get as a result of having additional responsibility, feeling important, feeling involved in decision making and leading others, dissipate and alternatives are sought out.

And then we get to the staffroom and complain that "these kids are so fidgety", or "they can't sit still, what's wrong with them?" Mistakes are perceived as high stakes sources of embarrassment instead of a necessary part of learning and those keen hands in the air start to dwindle until we're left with one or two pupils answering everything. Is this because we don't take the time to deeply explore a concept or misconception? Is it because we feel shackled by the week by week schema and the impending end of unit assessments in case our class is outperformed by another? Whatever the reason, it can't be because we prefer it that way, and we know the pupils certainly don't.

Have you ever asked your pupils or your children why they go to school? By this I mean exploring beyond "because I have to" or "so the school doesn't fine us", I mean *really* ask.

What are they hoping to get out of coming to school each day? If you stripped it all back to a blank page, what might they say?

Here we have a great opportunity to really get to know our pupils and find out what drives them . The following technique teaches some valuable future skills so don't be afraid to set aside 30 minutes to an hour once in a while...

Crazy 8s | A design thinking approach to learning and redesigning

Crazy 8s is a Design Thinking game or activity (but if you say it's a game they'll have more fun - Pavlov's Dog) that involves pupils working against the clock to come up with wild and barrier free ideas.

For this activity, each pupil will need a sheet of A4 paper, folded in half 3 times to make 8 squares on a side. Pupils put a small number 1-8 in the top corner of each box. *(alternatively you can use sticky notes)*

Grab yourself a Crazy 8s timer video from Youtube or just use your own timer. You're going to run 8 sessions of 40 seconds and pupils are going to jot down ideas.

You then pose a **How Might We** question.

How might we redesign our classroom to become a more flexible and inspiring learning space?

Here comes the craziness: There are no bad or wrong ideas! That's why we only give 40 seconds, long enough to jot down an idea but not long enough to talk yourself out of it.

The are only 2 rules:

1. When the 40 seconds is up you move on to your next box, even if you're not finished and if you finish before the 40 seconds you wait for the timer before moving on. In this way everyone is in the same mental space at the same time.
2. This is done in complete silence with no conferring or discussion

Once you have completed the 8 rounds, invite pupils to share their ideas with partners or groups.

*If you chose to use sticky notes, at this point you can ask pupils to start discussing and grouping the ideas based on themes they recognise

You can then hold a voting round where everyone gets 3 sticker dots and they circulate the room putting dots on their favourite ideas from their own or other people's Crazy 8s.

You then pull together the most popular ideas to formulate a picture of how you might redesign your learning space.

It's a great activity to encourage imagination, innovation and creativity whilst also teaching pupils to accept others' ideas, to leave their ego behind when getting feedback and to collaborate and agree on a plan. It also gives them a voice and ownership of the outcome. Regardless of whether their idea is used or not, they feel they have been involved in the decision making process.

So once you have some Crazy 8 ideas to start working with, you can begin to design a prototype alternative for user testing. This prototype might be in in the form of a topic, a period of time or even some A/B testing - in other words, doing the same thing in 2 different ways to see which is preferable or whether a hybrid of both works best.

This prototype should be by no means the finished article. The idea here, from the most popular ideas, is to settle on the 3 key features/functions you want the prototype to do. It should be a basic MVP (minimum viable process/product) that can be tested out by a number of users to gather feedback.
And away..., don't hold back, don't self-edit or procrastinate - get on with it and gather live feedback from pupils about the UX (User Experience). If anyone can be relied upon for honest feedback on teaching methods, it's the pupils so embrace it and leave the ego at home. They are feeding back on the reality, not the idea.

Once you've gathered sufficient feedback, take a step back and iterate, innovate, improve and then test again. It's a valuable process for everyone involved and goes way beyond the classroom, but it also means everyone has a stake in the outcome and a vested interest (some intrinsic motivation).

If pupils have designed their rewards, they are more likely to achieve them because they are dopamining in the right places, for the right things. Get the dopamine flowing in the right ways and the 4 Fs begin to disappear.

A common message

Another key component in pupil motivation, aside from relationships, which are of course, key, is understanding why our young people want to do well in exams.

Recently, in parliament, youth parliament member Izzy Garbutt made an impassioned speech and reasonable appraisal of the government's efforts to turn the education system into an exam factory. Her speech was based on her own personal experience and of course, it went viral.

Izzy said:

"The pressure students are under to perform is excessive, with the 2015 reforms in particular seeing an increase in content and more emphasis on examinations. Memorising has become a synonym for learning and mental health has suffered as a consequence. Wellbeing must become a priority and nurturing the development of young people as individuals should be the aim of education, not exam results."

Izzy is not alone in these experiences or opinions.

In 2017, the Association of School and College Leaders (ASCL) carried out analysis of reformed GCSEs and found that a pupil taking a typical set of these qualifications faced over eight extra hours sitting exams compared to under the previous system. In total, this amounted to 22 exams over a total length of 33 hours. Yes, 22 exams! In many cases, this also resulted in candidates sitting 2 or even 3 exams in a day due to clashes between exam board timetables.

Imagine waking up knowing you needed to be at school for 8am to sit an exam from 9 until 11, then sit in quarantine before starting your next one at 12, then sit a third in the afternoon session, finishing at 4pm. Good news, you get to go home to revise for your next exam in the morning.

Who does this approach help? Certainly not the students judging from the rise in mental health and wellbeing issues amongst examination aged young people. It also seems at complete odds with employers who constantly talk about the need for more emphasis on skills that equip young people for work and careers.

"We are pleading for more emphasis on employability, communication skills and personal wellbeing. Isn't the foundation of education creating well-rounded, well-informed young people ready for the future?"

*"Young people are more than just letters or numbers that they see on a piece of paper in mid-August. We are not a percentage of A*s to Cs, we are not evidence in an Ofsted report, and we are not a pass or a fail."*
Izzy Garbutt.

ASCL were also at pains to point out the plight of the 'forgotten third'.

This is the proportion of young people who do not achieve at least a Grade 4 pass in GCSE English and maths largely because the exam system is designed to determine how many pupils receive the respective grades.

Around a third of young people are therefore always likely to 'fail'* in qualifications which are a gateway to further study and careers. Pupils know and sadly, many accept that they have to fail in order for others to succeed.

*perceived fail of not achieving at least a grade 4

Talk about mixed messages! We spend earlier years telling young people they can achieve anything they want to, they can be anything they want to be and then, in their exam years we tell them that's only actually true for two thirds of them. We have a system where, if every single candidate scored 90%+, 33% of them would still have to fail because, them's the breaks.

*perceived fail of not achieving at least a grade 4

Recent studies on the Global workforce have found that despite claims of nonsense and scare-mongering, around 50% of the current school pupils will work in jobs that don't yet exist. As these jobs don't yet exist, the only way to prepare is to remain versatile, making sure your skills are transferable.

People will always be needed to do the things machines can't. The following qualities are considered valuable, whatever industry you end up working in:

- Empathy and Communication – Kindness, consideration and understanding are invaluable qualities
- Critical Thinking – Technology and Artificial Intelligence (AI) can predict variables, but we need human beings to make informed decisions
- Creativity – AI is great, but it can't create what doesn't exist. It relies on known variables, not dreams and inventions
- Strategic Thinking – Computers can map the small-scale stuff, but not the big picture

Earlier we mentioned some future jobs that are emerging. Here's a list of jobs that don't exist yet, but might do:

- Mind-Transfer Specialist
- Custom Body Part Engineer
- Robotic or Holographic Avatar Designer
- Gene Designer for Babies and Pets
- Extinct Species Revivalist

The Harris Poll, in conjunction with LEGO, surveyed 3000 pupils aged 8-12 in 2019 to ask what they want to be when they grow up. These were their responses.

I wonder how much those responses might have changed in the 3 years hence.

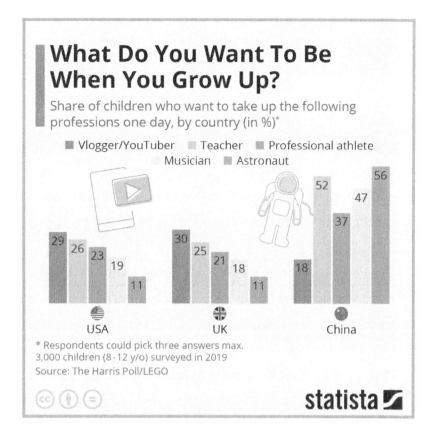

With job roles evolving and careers changing constantly, we need to ask ourselves "Why are we teaching what we're teaching?"

Why are we teaching what we're teaching?

There has been a welcome change in OFSTED's inspection framework in that there is now greater focus on curriculum intent alongside implementation and impact. Asking ourselves why we are teaching what we are teaching is now a growing part of curriculum design but the current system is still flawed in my opinion.

In 2011 the Wolf report was highly critical of the UK education system as it stood. Professor Wolf found that failures in the system "are not despite, but because of, central government's constant redesign, re-regulation and re-organisation of 14–19 education"

And that the "numerous examples of good quality innovation and success are achieved not **with** the help of our funding and regulatory system, but **in spite of** it…The priority must be to move 14–19 vocational education away from the sclerotic, expensive, centralised and over-detailed approach that has been the hallmark of the last two decades. Such a system inevitably generates high costs, long delays and irrational decisions".

More than 10 years later and employers and young people are still crying out for greater emphasis on skills. Yes, there has been a rise in apprenticeships but minimally so. The vast majority of school leavers do stay in the full time education system, developing knowledge as a priority through predominantly rigid, traditional methods as opposed to applied, vocational, skills-based options.

The reality in schools is that deciding what we teach is often based on a predetermined syllabus or prescribed curriculum that has either been designed or bought in from elsewhere.

Don't get me wrong, I'm not disparaging schools that have done this because this is more often than not a decision based on capacity in terms of time, knowledge and resources, but sometimes needs must. We need to get to a position where schools have the resources and capabilities to design an appropriate curriculum that is not only **challenging** but also **accessible to** and **relevant to** the pupil they serve whilst still being deliverable and sustainable.

It's well documented that in the UK, school leavers tend to progress more slowly in their first few years of employment than their OECD counterparts, largely because it is during this time that they are developing the skills needed to thrive in the world of employment. In a digital age where pretty much any fact can be Googled and so much of history is being re-written, knowledge of facts is of lesser importance than the ability to efficiently search, fact-check and present the information in an accessible way for the desired audience.

Let's be honest, if asked to give a report or presentation at work, how many of us would do so without getting a colleague to check it beforehand for ideas, questions that might arise and feedback? And yet, to our young people, all that 'appears' to matter in school is - Can you do it off the top of your head, in a room of silence with no assistance or collaboration?

So how do we make sure we are teaching the right things in the right way, whilst still having to align with our current examinations structure?

That's the killer question because it's the one that is about **OUR** pupils. What works for one primary school in the South West might not work at all for another in central Birmingham, but parts of it might. What works for a secondary in the North East might actually work for another in the South with a little adaptation.

Our curriculums need to be clear, accessible, flexible and fit for purpose, with that purpose being to enable all of our young people to develop the knowledge and skills they need to be successful in the future.

It's not about being successful in exams. It's about being successful in life because of the knowledge and skills gained in your formative years. School leavers who have sound transferable skills as well as knowledge will inevitably be more successful, whatever life throws at them because they will be better equipped to cope with challenges, set back and forge out new opportunities.

So given a blank canvas to design a curriculum, what would be our drivers?

Use this space to consider your own drivers for your school/subject/class.

Why not consider a design sprint with your colleagues to redesign your curriculum? Think not just about what needs to be learnt, but how to learn it in a way that allows skills to develop alongside the knowledge.

21st Century Learning

The 4 C's of 21st Century skills widely considered to be:

- Communication - sharing thoughts, questions, ideas, and solutions.

- Collaboration - working together to reach a goal, putting talent and expertise to work.

- Creativity - trying new approaches to achieve aims using innovation and invention.

- Critical Thinking - looking at problems in a new way and linking learning across subjects and disciplines. Looking beyond the surface.

These four skills are essential for people to succeed in the workplace and are therefore, essential for us to teach. I would argue that in some subjects, these skills are more essential than certain specific subject knowledge.

What does that look like for our pupils?

In order to build effective **Communication Skills** pupils must be taught to:

- Communicate using media and environments to support personal and group learning, including face to face and digital

- Share information efficiently and effectively using appropriate media and environments including face to face and digital

- Communicate thoughts and ideas clearly and effectively to a range of different audiences using a variety of media and formats

Today's pupils need to develop good collaboration skills, enabling them to:

- Work effectively with different groups of people, including people from diverse cultures.

- Be flexible and willing to compromise with team members to reach a common goal.

- Demonstrate responsibility as a team member working toward a shared goal.

Creatively Skills pupils must learn to:

- Use a range of idea creation techniques (such as mind mapping)

- Create new and worthwhile ideas

- Elaborate, refine, analyse and evaluate their own ideas in order to improve and maximise potential outcomes

- Act on creative ideas to make a tangible and useful contribution to the area in which the innovation will occur

And finally, Critical Thinking skills are essential in order to:

- Use different kinds of reasoning to understand a situation (eg through inference or deduction)

- Analyse complex systems and understand how their interconnected parts underpin the systems.

- Gather relevant information, asking the important questions that clarify points of view and help solve problems.

- Make decisions by selecting appropriate criteria and identifying alternatives to make reliable choices

These four C's enable our young people to create a whole that's greater than the sum of its parts. Combined, the four C's empower pupils to become one-person think tanks. Then, when those pupils get together, they can achieve almost anything. As long as we let them!

So, when planning our curriculum content and delivery, it's important to consider the skills just as much as the knowledge. Technology can be an essential tool to help deliver the learning outcome, but it is not learning in itself. We need to switch up out thinking.

What do we want our young people to do with the technology available to them?
Below is a simple sketchnote attributed to @PLUGUSIN and @RERDMANN that explains why that is the wrong question entirely.

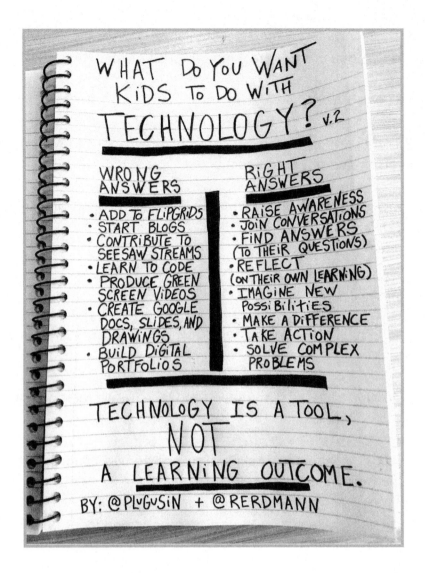

The where and when.

Once we have decided, through careful and critical thought, what skills and knowledge our pupils need to learn, it's important to then map where and when these fit into our curriculum model.

- Do we need to strip back and start from scratch?

- Is some of what we're teaching and learning hitting the mark?

- Do we just need to combine some newer ideas and approaches to existing content?

Whatever we decide, the production of a really detailed curriculum map poster to be displayed in every classroom means absolutely nothing if you don't live the intent. What's important is to consider the capacity of the pupils and staff.

Capacity, linked with the motivation we discussed earlier, falls into 2 categories: **general capacity** (do you have the skills and resources to achieve what's required?) and **innovative capacity** (do you have space in your brain after everything else to consider and process something completely new and groundbreaking, let alone implement it?)

This is why, when implementing change, it's vital to establish where your audience is at.

You may have a great strategy but limited capacity or motivation, which will probably result in failure.

You may have limited capacity but lots of motivation and the drive to make it work, probably resulting in success over time.

Ultimately, you need to have all 3 for the best outcomes, so consider this when planning to implement change. Ask yourself if it's the right time to do so. Is everyone exhausted at the end of term? Is everyone focused on exam season approaching? I know there is probably never an ideal time because the changing landscape of education (and its Ministers) is well-documented, but we must try in order to give ourselves a fighting chance of success. This goes for pupils as much as adults.

Once you've settled on the where and when, prototype it. Test it with one group as a control group to compare against others. Get feedback from staff and pupils about what worked and what didn't. Don't be precious about it, leave the ego behind and don't take it personally if people don't love it. Embrace the feedback as an opportunity to iterate and improve it further. Walk the walk that we talk with our pupils and demonstrate the skills we want them to develop.

Once you've gathered the feedback on iteration 1, it might be worth considering a Start, Stop, Continue discussion with stakeholders. It's as simple as it sounds, 3 questions;

- What should we start doing differently?
- What should we stop doing that's ineffective? (to enable us the capacity for the new things)
- What should we continue because it's working?

This is a powerful process to go through, especially with staff, as it gives the opportunity to get rid of things that are ineffective and therefore a pointless waste of everyone's time. Above all, be prepared to be flexible, which is why a digital document such as a spreadsheet is often easier than a flashy PDF, as you can easily adapt, resort and reorder the content based on the feedback you receive.

The hows

How we decide to deliver the content is just as important as what we deliver. The most interesting topics can appear dry if delivered in a way that doesn't stimulate. Now here, I want to be clear that I am not talking about 'edutainment'. I am a firm believer that challenge is all too often misbranded as boredom.

Maybe it's because our young people just aren't used to not being able to achieve things immediately, or at least get hints, tips and cheat codes immediately. They are growing up in a world where information is available to them 24/7 so they can find it alien when information is withheld or hidden.

This is one reason why I've always enjoyed organising very different, creative and challenging activities that take pupils out of their comfort zone. As Head of Sixth Form I used to organise a 3 day "Insight into Leadership" event where they would be put into teams, a little like The Apprentice, and be challenged to come up with and sell a product at a trade fair to the younger pupils. At the start, if I had had £1 for every student that mumbled the week before "I ain't coming, it's gonna be shit" I would have retired long ago.

The real joy for me would come about 90 minutes into the first morning where those who had 'voted with their feet' were getting calls from their team mates telling them to get their arses in because "it's really fun and we need you if we're going to stand a chance of winning".

Throughout the 3 days the teams would be faced with business challenges such as complaints to deal with, health & safety inspections and a range of team-building activities alongside some real unexpected curveballs to keep them on their toes.

The teams would have to pitch their product at the trade fair as well as keep track of their 'finances' before giving a presentation to the board at the end. Watching these young people grow during these 3 days was so rewarding and was often cited as one of their highlights of their time in Sixth Form.

This was 3 days off timetable, and there was certainly some resistance from staff who felt it was a waste of curriculum time, but we stuck to our guns and I'm so glad we did. Our Sixth Form served quite a deprived area (emotionally deprived rather than financially) and apart from anything else, it gave many of the students something tangible to talk passionately about at interviews. In fact, many of them would volunteer to come back and help coach teams in subsequent years!

I also love to create escape room type tasks for my pupils, the youngest of these being Year 7. Rather than end of unit tests I would often create digital breakouts to test my pupils' learning from a topic, wrapped up in a storyline. As a linguist, this was great as I could use different vocabulary as code to decipher or as locks to unpick with correct verb conjugation. I'd create these using a Google Form with response validation to proceed and then wrap it all up in a simple Google Site, slide deck or even a Thinglink.

Not only did students have to collaborate to use what they had learned but they were also, by default, self and peer assessing, problem solving, communication and thinking critically to understand how my weird brain works.

Not everybody loved it, but I'd group them so that they all had a fighting chance and some team members with resilience and determination to see them through. Competition is often a great motivator and I would often find those who were less forthcoming in a standard lesson would suddenly thrive in this environment.

Approaching, teaching or even assessing in different ways is fundamental to getting the best out of everyone. I only wish our exam system recognised this!

I was also flexible in terms of how work was presented to me, especially homework. I would give pupils the choice of how they would present their work, some would produce a piece of writing, others a slide deck, infographic, voice recording, and some even a fully edited video. Making use of awesome tools such as Mote, Flip (formerly Flipgrid), WeVideo and Screencastify opens up a world of opportunities for pupils to communicate in a way that suits them, whilst still maintaining the level of challenge.

Throw in the likes of Thinglink for VR opportunities and even AR and the world is your oyster. I'll never forget the day we were learning the names for animals in Spanish with Year 7 and we used AR technology on my phone to bring tigers and gorillas into the classroom, allowing pupils to get up close and personal with these lifesize digital creations. It's when you do something like this you often realise how much we, as adults, take for granted. When you hear pupils saying things like "I never realised tigers were that big" it makes you think - some of these pupils have never visited a zoo, let alone been on safari.

Another excellent example of bringing the world into the classroom is Google Arts and Culture. This amazing platform allows you to bring many art galleries in the world, and therefore some of the greatest works of art right there to their desks. Zooming in with Google Arts and Culture to Van Gogh's Sunflowers, you get closer and see more detail of the brushstrokes than you would if you were standing right in front of it.

Check it out below:

Sunflowers, repetition of the 4th version (yellow background), August 1889.[1] Van Gogh Museum, Amsterdam

Beyond artwork, Arts and Culture also allows you to explore different countries, try out experimental AI developments and more. One minute you can be standing on the Great Wall of China, the next you can be on the International Space Station before having some fun with the Blob Opera.

The difficulty I find, particularly in primary schools, is the amount of depth of knowledge that is now expected for an Ofsted Deep Dive. While primary colleagues are already expertly spinning numerous plates, they are now expected to be subject specialists too.

Equally in secondary schools, the teacher recruitment and retention crisis, along with rapidly decreasing budgets mean more and more teachers are teaching second, third or even fourth subjects as non-specialists. This puts a huge amount of extra work and pressure on those staff, but also on their department colleagues to support them. Planning takes longer, teaching is scarier, assessment takes longer, feedback takes longer.

This is where, when budgets won't stretch, we need to innovate in order to still deliver the content in a way that stretches, challenges and stimulates the pupils.

Here are some examples of creative solutions I have experienced in recent years.

- Collaborative Networks

Whether you are part of a Multi Academy Trust, a large school or a professional organisation, there are opportunities for professional networking if you seek them out.

I am fortunate to have been involved with the Global Google Educator Group (@GlobalGEG) and now co-lead @GEG_UK. During the height of the pandemic we were delivering training for teachers around the globe on all manner of things, almost 24 hours a day across the different time zones. We even ran online Google Educator boot camps for 10000 people.

The UK group is around 600 strong and made up of educators and school staff using Google for Education. There is also a twitter account and a Facebook page alongside a Youtube channel where we post helpful tutorials and live webinars.

These voluntary communities of individuals come together to solve the bigger problems, to crowdsource solutions and to share resources. The generosity of the people in these groups never ceases to amaze me.

This generosity can also be witnessed on social media, despite the scaremongering that often goes on around educators using social media. At the end of the day, use it responsibly and it can be an invaluable resource.

If you're on Twitter, check out some useful hashtags like:

#edutwitter
#FFBWednesday

and for the early risers amongst us
#Teachers5oclockclub

We are also seeing a growing trend in subject networks or focus networks across MATs as the opportunity to discuss and design at scale in order to gain consistency, reduce workload and improve impact are high on the list of priorities. What the last few years have shown is that these networking opportunities can often be just as beneficial remotely as they are in person.

Having said that, in person events are still fantastic and it's well worth booking your ticket for the Bett Show each year.

- **Specialists** (subject knowledge depth)

I am fortunate to sit on the academy council for an outstanding primary school in a very deprived area of Bradford and during a recent visit I was blown away by the progress being made in an area where historically, the attitude had been "what can you expect, we're in Bradford?". I've been on the receiving end of comments like that myself, when working in a school in special measures and it must be challenged.
I like the analogy of the flea in the jar.

If you're not familiar with this story, essentially when fleas are placed in an open jar they try to jump out. However, put the lid on and the fleas, hitting their heads on the lid, soon stop attempting the escape. They are being conditioned to the boundaries of the new environment they're in.

When the lid is removed, perhaps surprisingly, the fleas never jump out. Their thinking has created a metaphorical lid as the boundary, so has conditioned them to limit their jumping.

That's us as human beings - our thinking shapes us. It creates boundaries and limits ways of thinking that keeps us stuck in a certain routine or way of operating.

At this primary school, the leaders have invested in an innovative approach to teaching and learning. Firstly, each space is designed specifically for the age group for whom it provides. In early years for example, there are no chairs and desks, and as pupils progress, these are gradually introduced a couple at a time. This exposes pupils to the change at a manageable pace whilst also maintaining some level of stability and familiarity.

Much of the furniture is recycled, restored or donated and very little is traditional school furniture. The result is a very warm, inspiring environment with a range of spaces for different types of learning.

Aside from these space there is a museum gallery space (where local artists donate artefacts on loan to inspire pupils) and then specific subject specialist rooms. The school employs a range of specialists teachers in fields like Art, Music and Science in order to ensure the curriculum is delivered to the highest quality.

When not teaching, these specialists are support their colleagues in the best ways to deliver content with which they may be less familiar. The results are truly astounding and the artwork of Year 4 as an example is so mature and well explained that it could easily be mistaken for a Year 9 or 10's work. Partly, this is because the art specialist recognises that Art has a part to place in literacy and numeracy and works hard with pupils to study, discuss and verbalise their feelings and opinions on the work they create, as well as major pieces that inspire them.

This alternative approach means that the teachers feel more confident because they have specialists they can turn to and seek inspiration from, whilst the pupils make great progress because they feel valued, inspired, trusted and challenged.

- Forest School

"Forest School is a child-centred inspirational learning process, that offers opportunities for holistic growth through regular sessions. It is a long-term program that supports play, exploration and supported risk taking. It develops confidence and self-esteem through learner inspired, hands-on experiences in a natural setting."[1]

Forest School first arrived in the UK in 1993 and has grown extensively since then. My daughter loved it, especially getting muddy!

Forest School focuses on quality delivery, based around 6 unique principles:

1. Forest School is a long-term process of regular sessions, rather than one-off or infrequent visits; the cycle of planning, observation, adaptation and review links each session.
2. Forest School takes place in a woodland or natural environment to support the development of a lifelong relationship between the learner and the natural world.

---

[1] https://forestschoolassociation.org/what-is-forest-school/

3. Forest School uses a range of learner-centred processes to create a community for being, development and learning.
4. Forest School aims to promote the holistic development of all involved, fostering resilient, confident, independent and creative learners.
5. Forest School offers learners the opportunity to take supported risks appropriate to the environment and to themselves.
6. Forest School is run by qualified Forest School practitioners, who continuously maintain and develop their professional practice.[2]

- EELs (Extended Enterprise Learning)

At one of my previous schools, we were determined to make optimum use of the 20% curriculum time where we had some flexibility, but we didn't want to simply offer more of the same. As a staff we set about designing mini-courses that would serve 3 main purposes:
1. Provide unique learning experiences and pupil choice
2. Develop pupil skills beyond academic knowledge
3. Feel fun and unique to our school

Staff were given the licence to create and propose term-long courses that they were motivated to deliver. Pupils then had the choice to select courses from the list for each term of Year 7 and 8.

Staff were excited, if a little nervous at first, but were able to create courses using their wider skills beyond just subject knowledge. As a result we had courses covering things like Stage Make-Up, Go-kart building, Home skills and even Horticulture and Small Animal Care. I was responsible for the latter and we set up a mini-smallholding in an underused quadrangle of the school. As part of our lessons we learnt about our food and where it comes from, animal care and conditions as well as basic husbandry. We built flower beds, a chicken coop, created a pond for ducks and had challenges to see who could grow the most potatoes, as well as making our own butter and cooking and eating our own produce.

I was staggered by just how much the pupils loved getting hands on cleaning out the chickens and ducks or digging over the ground. They got really competitive over their seedlings and even learnt to furtle their potatoes.

Not only did this improve their engagement with the animals and plants, but also with each other. They became more tolerant, more patient and more empathetic, which undoubtedly had a wider impact.

_____

[2] https://forestschoolassociation.org/what-is-forest-school/

Whilst my pupils were looking after some rehomed battery hens, others were building and racing go-karts or trying out cool science experiments or learning how to cook and iron. We even got an article in a national magazine.

The main things were, pupil choice and pupil voice. Pupils had a chance to choose a course and if numbers were low for term 2, we knew it needed refreshing or replacing with an alternative. The advantage being we could consider anything. True innovation!

- PBL (Project Based Learning)

So PBL is nothing new, we've been 'doing projects' in schools since Moses was a lad. PBL in Secondary is a little newer though and again, one that teachers can often be wary of because it may feel unfamiliar. However, when planned and delivered effectively, it can give pupils the opportunities and confidence to try out and develop skills that otherwise they might not.

As a child, I was working with my dad every Saturday on the milk rounds, delivering milk and collecting the money. Believe it or not I started helping at about the age of 8. Around the same time I also joined the Cubs and later, the Scouts. My parents also ran the Venture Scouts section so when I wasn't working with Dad at weekends, I would often be away camping with Mum and the 16-18 year old ventures, fending for ourselves. I learnt a huge amount during that time and all of it practical. I was skilled with a knife by the age of 10 and an axe by the age of 14. I could canoe, row, cook, clean, erect a tent and build a bridge. I could tell you where North was from the trees and even build my own clay oven from recycled materials. I would have learnt none of that at school, but those are some of things that I remember most vividly, because I was proud. It gave me the dopamine boost that fed my desire for reward in an intrinsic way. The experience was reward in itself.

Can I tell you about any particularly memorable lessons at schools, aside from those ones with my English teacher, the answer is probably 2 or 3 max.
I do remember in Year 7 we were distilling alcohol and my Science teacher, Mr Francis, who was advanced in his years but a lovely guy, took a sniff and nearly floated off like Charlie with Willy Wonka's Fizzy Lifting Drinks.

Now, do I remember exactly what we learnt from that lesson? No. (unless you count not sniffing distilled alcohol)
Do I remember it because I had a good relationship with the teacher? Yes.
Do I remember it because it was funny? Definitely.

The other experience I remember well from school is that we used to go into school early on Fridays because my tutor was a PE teacher. We'd all head to the gym early to play volleyball during registration while all the other classes were doing something prescribed. We had such a laugh!

- Applied Digital Skills & CS First

Both of these programs, available free from Google for Education provide not only lots of ready made lessons and schema on a wide range of cross curricular topics but you can also select resources and lessons based on skills you want pupils to achieve.

The interface is very similar to Google Classroom but there are around 200 lessons along with plans, resources and videos ready to go. This means that pupils get to learn how to use digital tools in creative and imaginative ways at their own pace. They can watch a video several times, they can back and repeat, they can get support with their tasks all at the click of a button.

Applied Digital Skills in particular allows teachers to deliver important content for knowledge whilst simultaneously developing important future skills.

Here are just a few examples of the kinds of lessons or topics available from Applied Digital Skills.

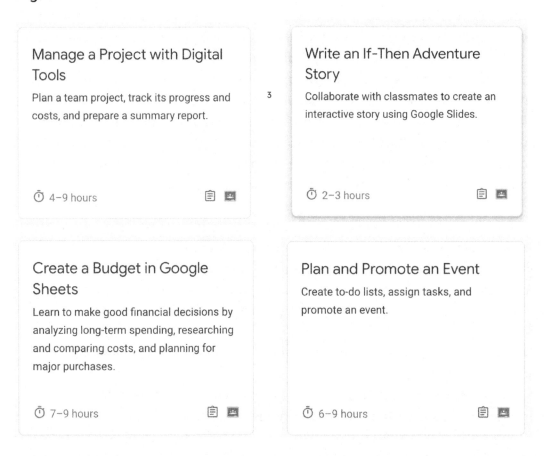

Manage a Project with Digital Tools

Plan a team project, track its progress and costs, and prepare a summary report.

Ⓣ 4–9 hours

[3]

Write an If-Then Adventure Story

Collaborate with classmates to create an interactive story using Google Slides.

Ⓣ 2–3 hours

Create a Budget in Google Sheets

Learn to make good financial decisions by analyzing long-term spending, researching and comparing costs, and planning for major purchases.

Ⓣ 7–9 hours

Plan and Promote an Event

Create to-do lists, assign tasks, and promote an event.

Ⓣ 6–9 hours

---

[3] https://applieddigitalskills.withgoogle.com/c/en-uk/curriculum.html

As you can see, they are really practical, real life citations - the kind of thing people complain "kids don't learn about in school".

So, what do these few examples have in common?

3 things: ***Play, purpose, passion.***

These innovative, and let's face it, sometimes risky approaches all encourage a sense of play and exploration, coupled with a clear purpose and relevance led by student choice and passion for a topic.

Forget written lesson objectives, WILTY, Starters/Mains/Plenaries, All/Most/Some and heaven forbid, VAK. If your curriculum, and your lessons can incorporate opportunities for those 3 things, you're on to a winner.

The who?

The key to any change process is obviously the people it directly affects, the stakeholders. I talked previously about motivation + general capacity + innovative capacity and being fundamental cogs in the innovation machine and that's as true for pupils as it is for adults.

One thing I would encourage all schools to do when implementing change is to consult and communicate. I don't mean put a letter on the website with a deadline and hope no-one sees it and replies so you can tick a box. I mean really talk, explain, show examples, perhaps even hold an event for parents where you can demonstrate your new idea.

Applied Digital Skills is a great example of this as you can invite parents in, get them set up and let them try it for themselves. They'll see how relevant and accessible it is, encourage their children and maybe even improve their own employability skills as part of the process.

When it comes to staff, it's not so much about training. Training for me is a one off thing, often not revisited. Coaching is where the impact lives. Regular, low stakes, honest and confidential support and challenge from a skilled coach will develop teachers far faster than any once a term INSET activity or 45 minute webinar.

Coaching is not widely experienced in the UK education system but it is on the rise. As a Google Certified Coach myself, I find the coaching process really useful, not just for working with others, but also for coaching myself at times. I often find myself stepping back and having an impartial word with myself about something that might otherwise feel quite personal.

The coaching process, done correctly can create a psychologically safe environment that encourages risk taking and innovation. Sadly, all too often in schools, rigid Performance Management based around pay awards creates the polar opposite. "If I admit I'm struggling with this, will I be put on a support plan and even more pressure?" is not a healthy place to be in one's mind. Contrast that with "I'll bring that up in my next session with my coach, perhaps we can come up with some potential solutions" and you get the picture. With coaching, you're in control, you choose the focus, you reflect on progress while your coach oils the wheels.

Coaching cycles might last 6 weeks to 12 weeks depending on circumstance but above all, interactions between coaches and coachees should remain confidential. Without this, there will be no trust and without trust it just won't have the desired effect for either party.

We want our teachers to feel part of this exciting journey and for their passion to show through, which means giving them the capacity to do it as well as the tools and confidence they need. Plan your implementation carefully, check against other priorities and demands and make sure you communicate clearly.

Whilst we are talking about coaching, and considering the example from Agora Schools, it brings me to secondary 'tutorial time' or whatever it may be called in your setting.

As a former tutor, Head of Year and head of Key Stage, it frustrates me to see tutor time being 'wasted' on a daily basis - and I've seen evidence of this in many schools. Sometimes it's down to lack of clarity or guidance, sometimes lack of skill, sometimes lack of interest. The one thing none of us were taught during teacher training was how to be an effective tutor and for some of us, it's the least favourable part of the job (ok, maybe second least after marking).

As a result, pupils often get a very varied experience depending on their tutor from day to day. I'm also confident that, despite claims that "there's nothing provided". That's more often than not down to a lack of knowledge or communication than a true claim. Usually, someone has taken on the responsibility of developing a tutorial program and is frustrated that people aren't using it consistently.

So how might we make better use of the time?

Some schools already run Maths, English and Science intervention classes during that time to support students who are underachieving or feel they need additional support. I applaud this but it takes some organising and requires Year 11 tutors to be teachers of those subjects, else a major impact on cover is often insurmountable. But what if we got rid of tutorial time altogether?

What if, during the course of a week, each pupil had a 1:1 session with their Success Coach who reviews their week with them, their goals, their issues and coaches them to move forward.

Each Success Coach could be responsible for 8-10 pupils and would meet with them weekly for 15 minutes. Some might say we can't lose that time from the curriculum but that's the point, you'd be gaining more than that back anyway. Plus, if we're delivering our teaching in ways that support learners working at their own pace, instead of the didactic teach from the front to everyone at once, the odd 15 minutes here and there will have minimal negative impact on their learning, and in all probability, significantly more positive impact overall.

Imagine the knowledge and relationship that could be established in this way, effectively providing each pupil with a life coach or guide. Think of the skills that would develop from a regular, detailed conversation with a coach who helped you process, repair and succeed.

It's just a suggestion, not one I've seen in action but I'd love to see it.

The evidence.

Ultimately, we live and work in an environment where written examinations have reigned for longer than her late Majesty Queen Elizabeth II, but times are changing.

Pilots are underway involving digital examinations in some subjects and more and more solutions are becoming available for in-class digital assessment.

If we look back at the concept of motivation, are pupils **really** motivated by exam results? Or are they conditioned to our 'motivation by proxy'? Of course we want our young people to succeed but we are obsessed with measurables because of tables and standards.

Given the choice of a miserable child with a sack full of 8s and 9s or a happy one with 3s and 4s, I know what I'd prefer, because I know that exam results don't define us. However, we routinely communicate the opposite to our young people when exam results decide our pay grade or job security. We impart our anxiety on to the very people who are least able to cope with it.

teachergoals

kids in 2050 trying to study the 2019-2022 chapter of history for a test

We obsess over measuring progress of quantifiables but through doing so, skew the results. In recent years, standards required at KS2 Maths have been equivalent to Year 10 or 11 with the same questions appearing both on the SATS papers as the GCSE and that's just one example.

The exam factory that Izzy Garbutt bemoaned in her speech to parliament is trundling along because no school can afford to take its foot off the pedal. Every school is in direct competition with its neighbour to get 'bums on seats' because they need the funding so collaboration between local schools is rare, despite them serving broadly the same communities.

It seems ridiculous to me that schools in one system, all supposedly working for the same goal, are then played off against each other every year, sometimes multiple times a year and boy, do the local press thrive on it!

Why do we do this to our young people, to our communities, to our Heads? We have a looming shortage of school leaders for the future, matched by a shortage of ITTs and ECTs so who exactly is going to be leading our schools in 10 - 20 years time?

Perhaps if we reconsidered our end goal, we might be able to break this cycle of doom.

LifeLong Learning

Hands up if you've still got one of these.

The National Record of Achievement was a folder given to secondary school pupils like me in the 1990s and early 2000s. It was a portfolio of poly pockets to house documents related to our academic and non-academic achievements, including GCSE certificates, school reports and anything else of relevance.

Adopted by the Department for Education in 1991, it was intended to allow us to demonstrate skills and achievements beyond our exam results, potentially of use for university admissions and to employers. We were told to look after it as we would need it and continue to add to it long after leaving school.

In reality, the National Record of Achievement was a damp squib. In fact, I have never been asked for it in the 30 years since I left secondary school.

The sentiment, for once, I think was right, but the implementation was not. In reality, after leaving school very few people went on to gain further qualifications where certifications were awarded and certainly not quickly enough to avoid the folder being lost in the loft or thrown out with a load of old tat from the underworld of the teenager bedroom.

If achieving and collecting successes throughout life was actually a thing, it might have worked, at least in some format. The rise in gamification shows that people, not just young ones, respond well to badges and accreditations. They like to add them to their CVs and their LinkedIn profiles, it's that intrinsic motivation popping up again.

It's not to earn more (although that would be nice), it's to demonstrate our skills to others, it's our desire for a dopamine rush when someone likes your latest update or endorses your skills to others.

I wonder how many people reading this even remember their GCSE results, or whether they have a rough guess when asked on an application form.

I struggle to recall my GCSE results, and I'm pretty organised with what I'd consider a good memory, however, I could reel off every 3rd party accreditation I've gained since becoming a teacher 24 years ago.

Why? Because in all honesty, my GCSEs don't matter any more. They did once, as did my A-levels and my Degree but since then not at all. Crazy really that the official final outcomes of 20 years of formal education essentially stopped being important almost immediately whilst those that some would call 'soft skills' are more important and valuable than ever.

So in this digital age, oughtn't we consider ditching end of course examinations for something else? "Egad!" I hear you cry, "that's a bit radical" but with today's young people expected to live to over 100, does it make sense that our worth is measured by exam results for the first 16 years only for it then to change? (at this point I have to admit being a little self indulgent, because I haven't heard anyone use 'Egad' in decades, but as a linguist with a love of words, I would love to see some of our lesser known historic vocabulary experience a revival in modern usage).

The resistance to using devices in lessons is often teachers worrying, because "in the end they have to hand write in the exam anyway" and you can understand why, but the tail is wagging the dog.

Take this scenario?

Pupil A exercise book:
Beautiful presentation, clear diagrams, colour coded with highlighters, perfect handwriting, notes of everything that was on the board.

Pupil B exercise book:
Presentation scruffy, only some handwriting legible, sketchy diagrams, notes partially copied from the board, some other scribbles or doodles

Who gets praised and who gets admonished in this situation?

I reckon 80% of the time Pupil A gets better 'feedback' than Pupil B but if we look a little deeper;
- Pupil A has spent a lot of time making the work very neat and attractive.
- Pupil A has copied notes verbatim from the board

- Pupil B has copied down some of what was on the board
- Pupil B has some scribbles that are hard to make out

What if those illegible scrawlings from Pupil B are really insightful thoughts, questions or concepts that you just can't read?

All Pupil A has done is copy existing content.

We're judging a fish by its ability to climb a tree.

How many people with immaculate handwriting go on to be GPs or surgeons?
I don't know the answer, but I suspect it's the minority.

Rewind.

Give both pupils the same access to devices, accessibility tools and the freedom to create some content to demonstrate their understanding and I guarantee you'll get very different outcomes.

Allow pupils to verbally record their answers to questions and you'll often get more content and clarity. Tools like Mote or Screencastify are ideal for this.

Allow pupils to sketch/design a solution and you may get a better understanding of their thought process than you ever would by asking them to write it down.

Equally though, for those who thrive on writing, we mustn't deny them that, it should be a personal choice and that may even change depending on the subject.

Microcredentials are great motivators as by their nature they are achievable in small, manageable chunks of time. You don't have to set aside 3 to 4 hours to complete your assessment, in some cases you can save your progress and return later. The key to that is asking the right sort of questions that require critical thinking and application, rather than factual knowledge.

I know, for example, that paracetamol will help me get rid of a headache, but I don't know exactly how. I do know that it lessens pain and therefore could be utilised to reduce pain in my toes just as much as it can in my head.

Imagine knowing what paracetamol does for a headache but not being able to establish, or even find out, whether that applies elsewhere. What's the point in having the knowledge if you can't apply it with the skills required?

So as we go through collecting microcredentials, the advantage is that these can quickly change and update and situations change. Some of the content I learnt as GCSE is now known to be incorrect because of more recent findings, but have I updated my GCSE? No. It's more dead than the Dodo.

A very high profile example of a dopaminer is heavyweight boxing champion, Tyson Fury. Tyson has been very open about his struggles with mental health and has famously retired and returned on numerous occasions. In Tyson's latest book, Gloves Off he talks at length about his battles with mental health, his need to have a goal and that that goal be relatively short term and achievable because long term goals don't motivate him, in fact, quite the opposite.

However, if I could 'top up' my credentials in areas that are relevant to my career, I might well choose to do so. Call it the mobile phone of qualifications, I've got a Pixel 6 and I'm due an upgrade soon, but do I go for a 7 or wait a bit for the 8? That's a decision I can make for myself once I've seen what the 7 offers me and if it's worth the investment.

The same could be said of credentials. What does the update offer me and is it worth investing my time at this point? Would my time be better invested elsewhere? And what if these credentials recognised skills as well as knowledge as equals?

The Education Design Lab is a nonprofit organisation, based in the US, that has been championing the value of microcredentials for quite some time. having developed their own microcredentials to demonstrate to employers that students have mastered certain soft skills, including critical thinking, oral communication and creative problem-solving.

Don Fraser Jr, The Education Design Lab's chief program officer, argues that higher education often needs to be spurred to quickly transform, such as through a pandemic, tragedy or public embarrassment, and the same is true of compulsory education in the UK.

"Higher ed can't keep doing what they're doing and expecting the world of work to be OK with it,"

"They're starting to look at other forms of credentialing," [and] *"This puts institutions in a good position to be able to deliver on that."*

Can we say the same about schools?

Many companies have been promoting their own microcredentials, including Coursera, an online course platform, LinkedIn and even edtech startups like Edpuzzle have created their own teacher learning library.

Microcredentials could help make the job market more equitable for students who don't go to top-ranked universities or even Further Education, but pursue a more vocational route.

Increasingly, it's becoming less about where you went to school/ university and more about whether or not you have the skills. Microcredentials can allow people to showcase their skills and accomplishments in different ways.

Instead of encouraging pupils to create dull A4 word document CVs, perhaps we should be getting them creating living, breathing eportfolios to showcase not just their credentials, but also their creations, examples of their work, video endorsements from others and more.

These stand a chance of living on and adapting with time instead of being found in 30 years at the back of the old wardrobe covered in dust and dead spiders.

So in a world with so many options in terms of educational technology, how do we know where to start, where to invest and where to cut our losses?

Of course we could ask our stakeholders, our teachers and our pupils, but this might produce biassed results as people only know what they know. I've often had conversations with pupils and colleagues who have a gripe about something they don't like, but when asked, they don't really have any idea of the alternatives available. They just know they don't appreciate the status quo.

For this reason, it's important to look beyond our own walls and utilise wider networks to explore, enable, empower and energise your community.

Any change in operational habits, small or large, requires careful planning and implementation, both with adults and children and the necessary behaviours of success need to be modelled and taught.

This process of change will likely be embraced by some and avoided by others. When it comes to change, humans of any age are funny. I like to think of them as characters from Winnie the Pooh. Let me explain.

Pitch a new approach or idea to a room full of people, of any age, and you'll undoubtedly experience a mix of the following.

Firstly, around 5% will be **Tiggers.** These are your innovators who can't wait to get started. They're enthusiastic about the new opportunity and bounce around getting very excited.

Secondly, you'll have somewhere between 5-20% who are **Poohs,** your early adopters who are keen to embrace the new approach but fairly level headed. They might dip their toe in the water but they'll want to see what the Tiggers' experience is like before they completely commit. Getting enough of these Poohs to commit and promote your approach is key to bringing the later groups along on the journey.

Next, come the keener amongst the main population, the **Piglets** who are happy to go along with it if others believe in it. They put up little resistance to new ideas and your early majority.

Then, you'll find another 20% -30% who are your late majority. These are those who are reluctant and really not convinced. These **Eeyores** will hold back and put it off until they absolutely have to do it, but can be convinced if the Tiggers and Poohs are sharing positive experiences. They are always the ones you have to chase.

Finally, you'll have the remaining who are you **Owls**. These individuals have been there, seen it, done it, bought the T-shirt and outgrown it. They've seen it all before with another name and are not for turning. Any amount of effort on your part will have negligible effect, if any at all and while you're busting a gut with these laggards, you could be having a greater impact on those above.

I know this may be controversial to some but in my experience, you won't change these Owls, they'll only change if they want to, and no amount of your effort will change that. If and when they do accept the new approach, they'll rarely admit it was because they were wrong or that you were right. Don't waste your time - if you have confidence in your approach and the majority is on board, those laggards can join the party or get off the bus altogether. Ultimately, everyone has a choice.

This analogy could also be explained using the widely accepted product adoption curve, but I prefer the character approach to a simple quantifying label.

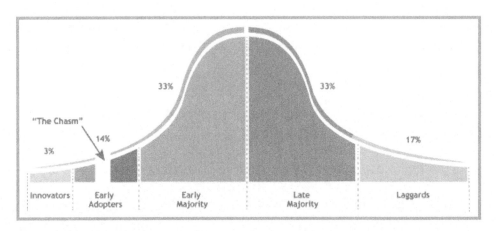

Another great visualisation of the change management process can be seen in a video that can be found on Youtube called "The First Follower" from Pioneering Leadership.

This excellent 3 minute video about process adoption, begins with a lone dancer, who is stared at by passers by until he is gradually joined by individuals that see what he is trying to achieve and are prepared to stand out and join in, accepting the risk that they may look silly.

It's these first followers, not the lone dancer, that make it socially acceptable for others to 'join in'. They feel psychologically safer as the risk of embarrassment is reduced. The more people that join in, the faster the group grows until almost everyone is up and dancing along.

This parabolic adoption curve is to be expected but careful planning before implementation can help to accelerate the early stages and therefore the entire process.

Often, individuals that make great 'first followers' don't make great leaders and vice versa. The leaders or lone dancers are the quick decision makers, they make a decision based on the information they have in front of them and go for it.

First followers on the other hand, will often pontificate over decisions but once a decision is made by the leader, they are more than happy to support and make it happen.

Both types of people are vital in any successful team, be that in professional life or classes. Each one relies on the other in order to be successful. A decisive leader with no followers quickly becomes a dictator without stakeholder buy in. A first follower with no-one to follow is easily lost despite a willingness to move forward.

Our goal in schools and beyond is to make our intentions clear, in order to be kind. We must communicate what we want to achieve, why we want to achieve it and what we will gain from it and how we aim to achieve it, bringing us neatly back to the 3 Ps I mentioned earlier: Play, Purpose and Passion.

In the next section I'll highlight some of the amazing tools I would recommend, along with potential use cases.

3rd Party Tools To Enhance The 4 C's

It ought to go without saying now, following 2 years of the Edtech Demonstrator Program and a voyage of discovery for many, that the main choice for schools in the UK is Google for Education or Microsoft.

Both have their merits and their faults but ultimately, the key is to focus on the principle rather than the product. Many of the products mentioned in this section have options to integrate with a number of other tools and platforms so the choice is very much yours, or your school's. All of the tools mentioned here are available for FREE in some format but may also have further subscription versions.

Interactive Lesson Resources with Formative Assessment Options:

Genially - rapidly growing in popularity in the UK, Genially offers interactive, animated and dynamic templates to support content delivery in any subject.

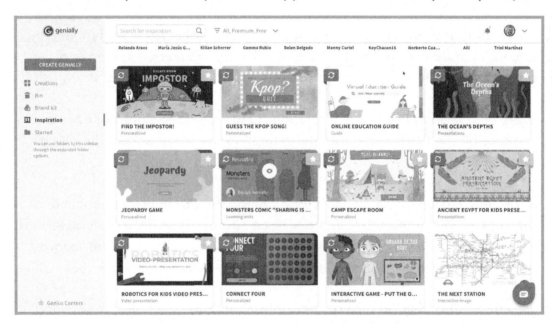

There is an extensive Inspiration gallery where educators and creators from around the world have shared their creations for inspiration and adaptation, as well as creating your own from scratch if you feel ready. The Inspiration gallery contains all manner of templates from slick presentations, to if-then adventure stories to digital escape rooms.

Edpuzzle

Throughout lockdown I used Edpuzzle extensively. The features allowing me to use video to engage pupils remotely were a huge bonus and they have continued to improve. Edpuzzle allows you to use ready made content, content from Youtube or upload your own video content and add comprehension questions really easily. Questions can be multiple choice (with automated marking) and open ended (requiring teacher assessment) and then teachers get a breakdown of how much of the video each pupil watched, how many times they watched it and how many attempts they took to get the answer correct.

Feedback can be added to answers to extend or address misconceptions, and my favourite aspect - if pupils try to minimise the window, the video stops. There's no 'watching it in the background' with this cool platform.
Edpuzzle have recently added options to screen record natively and also for pupils to respond and submit videos of their own.

Single users can house 20 videos for free, but share with others and your quota rises. Schools and MATs can even set up shared libraries where teachers can share and inspire each other. Edpuzzle also has a great bank of CPD micro-courses available for teachers on all manner of teaching and learning related subjects.

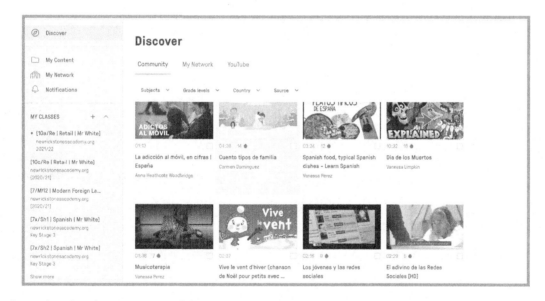

Edpuzzle also integrates with many LMS (Learner Management Systems) such as Google Classroom to pull grades into your gradebook effortlessly.

Quizlet is another tool that can help make learning and assessment fun and engaging. Providing a variety of modes including games, study sets, flashcards, quizzes and even Live options, Quizlet also

offers an expert area with a huge range of ready made resources for you to use.

My students particularly enjoyed a Live end of lesson horse race to check their learning. The frustration being you could be out in the lead but get an answer wrong and you're pegged back!

Nearpod offers another video based option, again with huge ready made resources as well as the option to make your own, along with a Google Slides add-on to turn existing slide decks into engaging self or teacher paced content in minutes.

Nearpod allows you to set all manner of questions to pupils, based on content you share within the Nearpod itself. That might be text, images, video, sound, you name it and then you are able to set questions, tasks or challenges to check understanding and help you address misconceptions. Every pupil can even get their own whiteboard that you can then oversee and share with the class for further discussion.

The Nearpod library offers lots of inspiration and ready to go content, you can clone and adapt existing content or upload your own. You can deliver live during the lesson with everyone going at the same pace or you can allow pupils to work at their own pace, all the while able to monitor where they are up to as well as how well they are scoring in any low stakes assessment elements such as multiple choice questions, open ended questions or even drawings and diagrams.

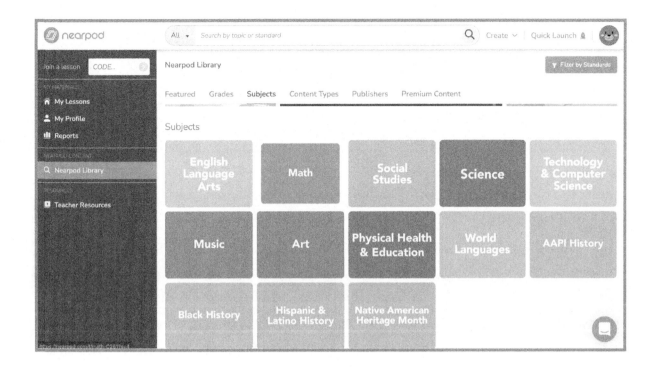

Collaboration & Creative Resources:

Jamboard from Google, apart from being an impressive piece of hardware, also has 2 software formats available; an android app and a web solution, meaning it can be used on any device.

Jamboard is a clean, simple collaborative whiteboard solution tool that integrates with Google Drive and also works in a Google Meet video call. Tools on the web version include pens, highlighters, sticky notes, add images, shapes and text.

The android app boasts additional features including handwriting recognition and conversion to text as well as smart drawing aids, meaning everyone can create impressive and clear sketchnotes, diagrams or scenes.

Up to 50 people can collaborate on a jam at any one time with a maximum of 20 frames (slides). You can even add your own images as backgrounds but by far may favourite was to add instructional GIFS to the background so pupils could review a process on a loop if they needed to do so, freeing up my time to support students rather than explaining and reexplaining a concept.

To get started with your first Jam, just type **jam.new** into the omnibox and enjoy!

Miro is another fantastic collaborative tool with an infinite canvas. Similar in concept to Jamboard but infinitely more equipped, Miro allows all sorts of collaborative work including planning, reviews, smart meetings, mindmapping, ideation and much more. There is a huge gallery of templates that you can use and adapt or you can choose to start with a blank canvas. There are tools to embed 3rd party documents and features as well as in-built video call, comment and presentation modes plus voting, timers and background music to add to the fun. Miro is now also available from within a Google Meet as a tool.
This screenshot is from a session I ran with a Year 6 group on Digital Safety. Although it looks busy, it's actually a sequential series of frames (slides) and all those red dots are pupils adding their own thoughts and reflections on each frame.

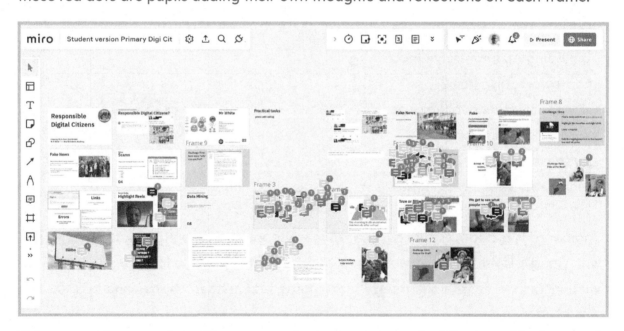

This was a 1 hour session with a group who had never used a Miro board before, and as you can see, they really got stuck in.

Padlet is a versatile platform for gathering and sharing information from a variety of sources. Once you create a padlet it can be shared for others to access and edit or view. Users are then able to like, upvote and comment on added content that can include text, images, videos, urls and more. It's a great way to crowd source opinions for review, and because you have the option to use moderation, nothing need appear on the live view until you approve it.

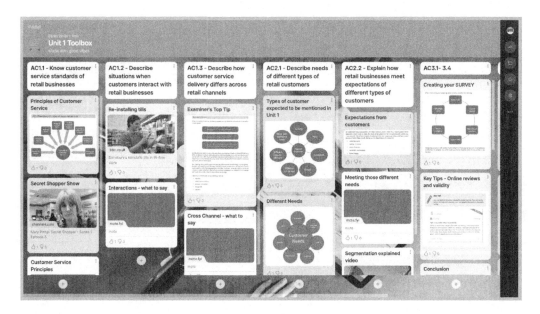

Knowledge Organiser for KS4 Retail Business

Crowdsourcing Padlet where pupils found examples of advertising fails and then had to vote on the worst, explaining why. This is the teacher view, notice the pink **Approve** buttons for posts pending moderation.

Other use cases that have been really popular include:
- a Year 11 Leavers' Padlet where staff and parents were invited to share messages to our school leavers,
- Roadmaps for ideas sharing and communicating what's in development with a product or process.
- PE headlines Padlet with photos and results from fixtures.

SCAN ME

The great thing is that the viewable Padlet can be embedded directly into a website too.

Figma is another great tool for design and collaboration. A little more business focused, it has the benefit of allowing wireframing and prototyping mockups with which to gather feedback. However, growing in popularity is the FigJam feature which offers similar options to Miro.

Once again, there are a plethora of templates, and when you're a busy teacher, that means a lot. ⬤

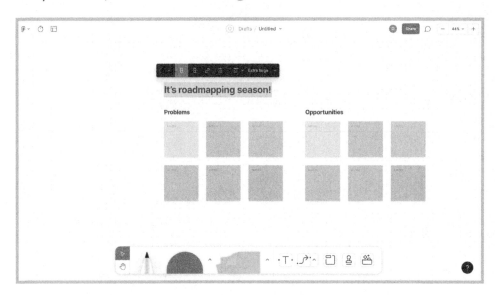

Above: A blank roadmap FigJam   Below: FigJam Template Library

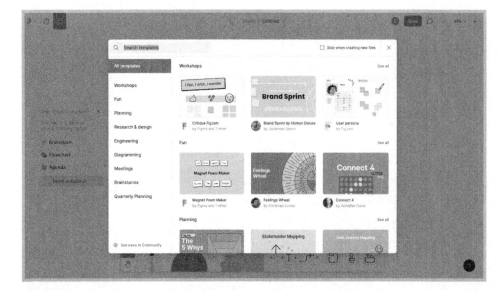

Canva might not have featured in this section until very recently but with the recent addition of collaborative projects in Canva, it simply can't be missed out.

Aside from being a fantastic platform for any sort of design or marketing content creation, it's also fantastic for creating collaborative presentations, videos and more. An added bonus is that all teachers are eligible for a FREE Canva for Education account, which offers additional features and content to the free version.

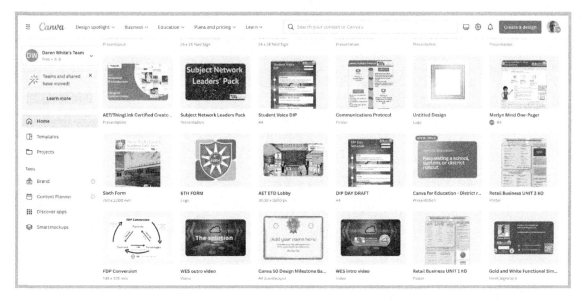

You can create your own teams and share projects amongst you for input and quality checking and feedback before publishing.

Communicational Resources:

Mote is undoubtedly one of my favourite apps, having discovered it during the first lockdown. Mote allows you to record voice notes and quickly add them to comments, webpages, slides and more to share accessible, personalised feedback.

After a few weeks of using Mote I realised that a class set of work that took around 2 hours to mark by hand, was only taking around 30 minutes using voice comments with Mote. Not only that but the quality of the feedback was improved too, I think, because it felt more personal and less repetitive.

Mote has grown since then and there are some tremendous features including transcription of a comment, translation, reactions and feedback loops between teachers and students. Mote's tagline is "Type less, talk more" and I think that's something we can all get on board with. Aside from anything else, the verbal nature of the feedback means tone and accent can also be conveyed to help convey the message, that might not always communicate in writing.

Furthermore, you can access all your recording from one dashboard and even see if the comment has been read and/or listened to.

Mote lets you access all your recordings and see who has heard/read them

Video tools:

The following video tools are all web-based and therefore device agnostic, meaning you can use them on PC, Mac or Chromebook as well as on iOS or Android in some cases. They are also freely available with paid upgrades, although completing the linked microcredentials can open up exclusive packages.

Flip Previously known as Flipgrid, **Flip**, from Microsoft is an educational take on video socials like TikTok. Principally used on mobile devices, but available as a web version, Flip allows teachers to set video assignments and pupils can respond with video, voice, emojis & fun but 'healthy' filters. Teachers can set time limits, respond to submissions, share them with other pupils for peer assessment and even create their own 'mixtapes' of their favourite content to share wider.

This is a great tool for encouraging pupils to share their understanding and thinking, and particularly useful for MFL teaching. Another great use case is for Primary to Secondary transition, where pupils can record video introducing themselves to their new teachers, including how to pronounce their name, what they enjoy and what sorts of things help them in class.

Flip teacher dashboard with all topics, pupil responses, assessment and more...

The following 3 options allow very simple and quick screen recording of your own screen or from your webcam, or both making them perfect for recording your thinking, explaining a concept or creating asynchronous content for pupils.

All have free options with time limits but paid versions are available that extend those limits and add further features including editing, blurring and more.

Screencastify	Loom	Wevideo

Canva and Adobe Express also offer a very simple video creation tool for less complicated outcomes, although no less engaging and professional-looking.

Micro-learning & PBL style Resources:

SCAN ME

<u>**Book Creator**</u> is a fantastic tool that can be used by pupils of all ages, as well as teachers. Create your own books and workbooks for your pupils to use or get them collaborating on stories or non-fiction books of their own.

There is an extensive library of books published by other authors worldwide, sorted by subject and age group and this is a brilliant source of inspiration. One of the advantages of Book Creator is that you can incorporate a wealth of multimedia content including videos, sound, maps, images and more.

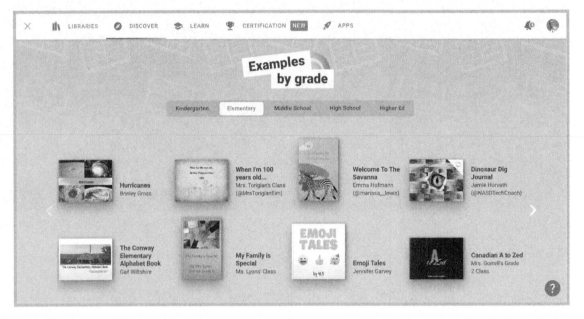

Book Creator Discover

From: When I'm 100 years old, by Mrs. Torigian's Class (@MrsTorigianElm)

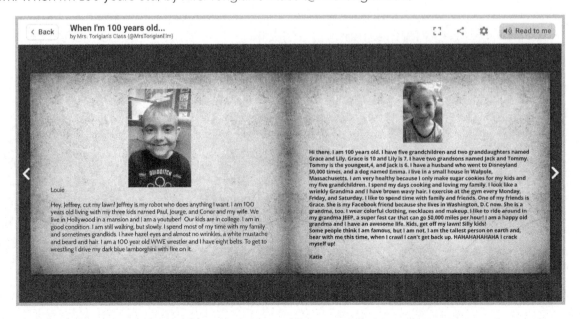

In this example (use the QR code for a better look) I love how the pupils have used an ageing app for their photos and been really imaginative about what they might be like at that age.

Applied Digital Skills (UK) as I have already mentioned in previous chapters, also provides a project-based learning approach to digital skills through cross-curricular routes.

Its partner, CS First offers the same for Computing without the need to be a complete coding expert thanks to the video guides and supported plans and resources.

Artificial Intelligence Resources:

Quillbot is another resource being used more and more in the workplace and of course, in school or at home by pupils. It allows you to enter text and have the bot paraphrase the content based on a certain audience. It will come as no surprise that this is widely used to copy existing content and convert it into "your own words" to avoid plagiarism checks.

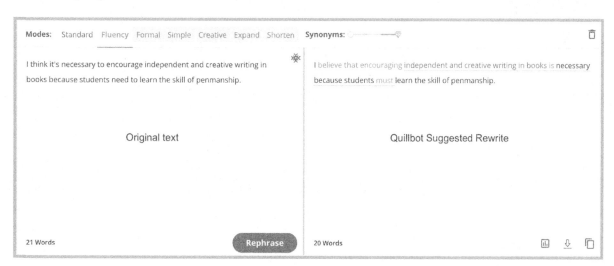

It certainly challenges our current approaches and makes us think about the reality of the 'real world' that we are supposedly preparing our pupils for.

Conker

New off the blocks from the creators of Mote, Conker enables users to drop text and have AI generate comprehension questions based on the content in seconds. Teachers can keep or edit these generated questions and even add custom feedback for correct/incorrect answers and export them straight to a Google Form in an easy click. This will save a huge amount of work for teachers and also allow them more time to analyse the results of the questions and take appropriate action to address misconceptions or gaps, rather than wasting time marking manually.

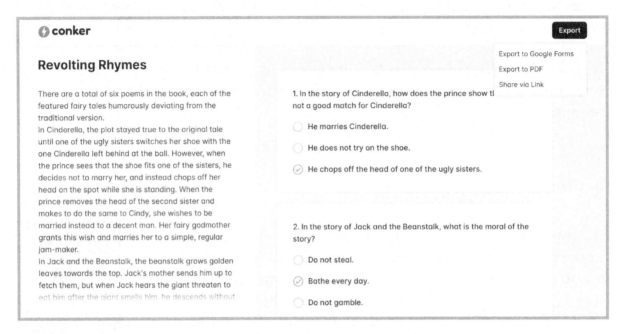

A precis of Revolting Rhymes by Roald Dahl, with AI generated comprehension questions.

Merlyn Mind

Merlyn is the first Voice Assistant for the classroom. Hook up to your computer and screen and ask Merlyn to perform the tasks that interrupt your teaching, the mundane. Commands like:

"Hey Merlyn, open my presentation on Planets" and Merly will find it and open it on screen.

"Hey Merlyn, start a timer for 5 minutes"

"Hey Merlyn, go to tab 4" to bring forward another tab.

All of this and more can be done from anywhere in the room, and you can even let the pupils do it too.

You can isolate the sound to just your voice via a small remote, but you also allow pupils to ask Merlyn questions, allowing you the freedom to circulate the room and support others.

In my class, the pupils loved Merlyn, probably more than I expected. I wasn't convinced they would go for it being 14 year olds, but before long they were stroking and greeting Merlyn when the entered the class and I even 'caught' some less focused pupils suggesting to each other that they "ask Merlyn because Sir is busy with X over there".

I know there may be some scepticism but don't knock it till you've tried it! It is after all, the way many of us operate around our homes.

Confession: I do enjoy the ability to ask my Google Assistant to boil the kettle when about 5 minutes away from home after a busy day.

Confession 2: Ernie the Dachshund has become tuned to Google's voice and knows when it speaks and says it's "turning Ernie's fire on". He only has to hear it and he's making a beeline for the fireplace.

A Declaration:

"The most effective way of teaching is to use a variety of methods that are tailored to the needs of the students and the subject matter being taught. This may include using hands-on activities, collaborative learning, and using technology to engage students and enhance their learning. It is also important for the teacher to create a positive learning environment that is conducive to learning, and to regularly assess and adjust their teaching methods to ensure that students are understanding the material.

Assessment should be conducted in a way that is fair, valid, and reliable, and that accurately measures the students' knowledge and understanding of the material. This may include using a variety of assessment methods, such as quizzes, tests, projects, and assignments, to get a well-rounded view of the students' abilities. It is also important for the teacher to provide clear, specific, and timely feedback on the students' performance, and to use the results of the assessments to inform their teaching and improve student learning.

Regardless of the method used, it is important for the feedback to be specific, timely, and actionable, so that the student knows exactly what they did well and what they need to improve. In general, it is best to provide feedback as frequently as possible, so that students have the opportunity to use the feedback to improve their performance. This may mean giving feedback on a daily or weekly basis for some activities, and less frequently for others."

At this point I'd ask you to consider how much you agree or disagree with the above declaration. You could use the table below to note down your thoughts.

Reasons to agree	Reasons to disagree

Next, I'd like you to think about the perspective of the author. What kind of person would have written this? Again, feel free to note some ideas below.

And now the reveal. The declaration above was written by ChatGPT, an AI powered bot that generates content based on prompts. In this case, the prompts were 3 questions:

1. What is the most effective way of teaching?
2. How should assessment be conducted?
3. What methods of feedback are most effective and how often should feedback be given?

These questions took less than 30 seconds to write and the results took about the same length of time to generate.

So, how do you feel about that? Does it astound you, worry you or frustrate you? What does it say about the future of teaching and learning and examinations?

Given the choice, would you always, sometimes or never use a tool like this?

I freely admit there would be times when I'd be reluctant, but others where it makes complete sense, both in terms of effort, time and cost. In a fast-paced world where deadlines are tight and content needs updating regularly, why not automate some of that process, even if only as a starting point?

Collation Resources

Wakelet is a perfect solution for collating resources, examples of work, inspiration images, pretty much anything online that you want to collate.

Personally, I love to use Wakelet for mood boards when decorating at home but it's also great for sharing resources around a topic or showcasing great examples of work or images.

I also use Wakelet to pool resources for training sessions and courses I deliver so everything is in one place, but can be quickly and easily added to using the chrome extension.

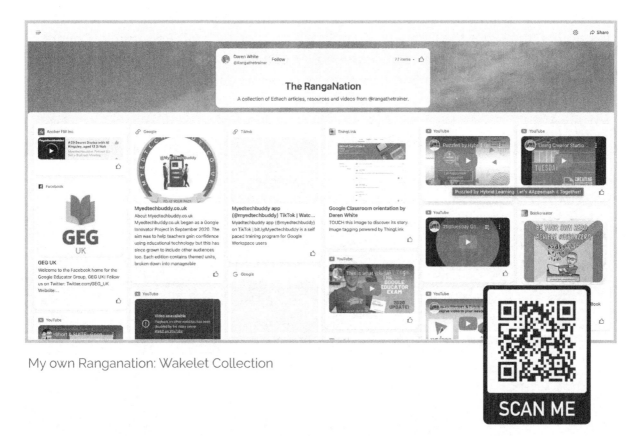

My own Ranganation: Wakelet Collection

Google Sites

If you're looking for a similar solution that isn't publicly available on the web, Google Sites are super easy to create and adapt, but need only be published internally within your domain.

This keeps an element of control over content and is particularly helpful with regards to consent for use of photographic images.

Other equivalents to this than can be shared privately include **Adobe Express Pages** and **Microsoft Sway**.

And finally, Thinglink

"Thinglink is an award-winning education technology platform that makes it easy to augment images, videos, and virtual tours with additional information and links. Over 4 million teachers and students use ThingLink for creating accessible, visual learning experiences in the cloud" is what it says on their website but that really doesn't do it justice.

Not only does Thinglink allow real time exploration on desktop, it also allows use of VR headsets for fully immersive experiences that pupils might not otherwise get.

Super easy to use with questions options and conditional transitions from one frame to another, the sky is the limit with Thinglink. Any image 2D, 3D Panoramic, Sphere or even GIFs can be used as a background for a Thinglink, to which you can add all manner of 'tags' to link content, information, websites, forms, you name it!

Personally, I've used it with great success for digital escape rooms, onboarding for staff and students around tech tools, knowledge organisers to name just a few.

You can even explore 3D images of every day or specialist objects in close up detail. Check out the **Thinglink Blog** for inspiration

Conclusion

I hope you have enjoyed reading this as much as I enjoyed creating it. I also hope it has made you think.

My intention is to stimulate thought, debate and innovation as we move ahead further into the 21st Century. It is very clear that a new way of working is here to stay in some format, whether that be fully remote or hybrid.